Radically
Happy

Radic...

H...

Shambhala
Boulder
2019

A user's guide to the mind

PHAKCHOK RINPOCHE

and

ERRIC SOLOMON

Illustrations and design by
JULIAN PANG

Shambhala Publications, Inc.
4720 Walnut Street
Boulder, Colorado 80301
www.shambhala.com

9 8 7 6 5 4 3 2 1

First Paperback Edition
Printed in the United States of America

⊗ This edition is printed on acid-free paper that meets the
American National Standards Institute Z39.48 Standard.

♻ Shambhala Publications makes every effort to print on recycled paper.
For more information please visit www.shambhala.com.

Shambhala Publications is distributed worldwide by
Penguin Random House, Inc., and its subsidiaries.

Designed by Julian Pang

THE LIBRARY OF CONGRESS CATALOGUES THE HARDCOVER
EDITION OF THIS BOOK AS FOLLOWS:

Names: Rinpoche, Phakchok, 1981– author. | Solomon, Erric, author.
Title: Radically happy: a user's guide to the mind / Phakchok Rinpoche and
Erric Solomon; graphics by Julian Pang.
Description: First edition. | Boulder: Shambhala, 2018. |
Includes bibliographical references.
Identifiers: LCCN 2017049452 | ISBN 9781611805277 (hardcover)
ISBN 9781611807691 (paperback)
Subjects: LCSH: Buddhism—Psychology. | Happiness—Religious Aspects—
Buddhism. | Mindfulness (Psychology) | Meditation—Buddhism.
Classification: LCC BQ4570.P76 R56 2018 | DDC 294.3/444—dc23
LC record available at https://lccn.loc.gov/2017049452

*May our precious teachers' aspirations for
the welfare of beings swiftly come to pass.*

*May all be free from suffering and
have all the causes for radical happiness.*

*This book is dedicated to the contentment and
well-being of everybody, everywhere.*

CONTENTS

FOREWORD

I f we look within ourselves with some perspective, we might see how our mind can be like a wild monkey. Left to its own whims, the mind can, in an instant, take off in any direction—here one second, there the next.

How can we take more control?

Operating manuals for the mind have existed for millennia, particularly in Asian cultures. These have been meditation instructions—pithy bits of advice for the monks, nuns, and yogis who devoted their lives to these practices. Typically secret, they were not shared beyond the small circle of these hard-core practitioners.

Fast-forward to the twenty-first century. Brain scans of Olympic-level meditators show how much their minds have shifted in beneficial ways from this inner workout; meditation, it turns out, operates like a mental fitness workout. And neuroplasticity explains how working a given mental circuit, the essence of meditation practice, makes those neuronal links stronger. The data points to a dose–response relationship, where the more time you put in, the stronger the benefits are. And these show up from the very start.

The need has never been greater. Since these ancient methods were first practiced, everything has changed. Indeed, the sheer velocity of change—social, technological, cultural—escalates hourly, it seems, a torrent that demands we continually adjust to newness. Our heads spin.

So it's no surprise that millions now seek some inner peace through the pursuit of meditation. This mental workout comes in a myriad of forms, some highly effective, others not so. But meditators or not, we all need an easy-to-use, pragmatic operator's manual for the mind.

You've found it here.

Consider the authors. We've known them both for many years and can attest to the depth of their knowledge and their empathy with our predicaments.

Phakchok Rinpoche hails from a long line of meditation masters. His grandfather Tulku Urgyen was one of the greatest meditation masters to emerge from old Tibet in the 1950s. And Tulku Urgyen's great-grandfather Chokgyur Lingpa was legendary throughout nineteenth-century Tibet as a revealer of great wisdom teachings. Phakchok Rinpoche himself was recognized as the reincarnation of yet another great Tibetan master.

And yet, as you'll see in *Radically Happy*, Phakchok Rinpoche lives much like the rest of us and so can draw on his own doubts, anger, and other familiar feelings to illustrate ways we can each find steadier footing in the rocky realities of our lives. His earthy tales of dealing with life's stuff mix with his remarkably clear and accessible instructions—heart advice for navigating the tricky shoals of our own mind.

Erric Solomon adds a different wealth of expertise. Mastering the craft of software writing at a young age, he spent years as an executive in the high-pressure world of Silicon Valley. At the same time, Erric Solomon became a serious practitioner of Tibetan meditation. He speaks in the no-nonsense voice of a techie but with the clarity of a seasoned practitioner, presenting mind-training methods in a way that resonates with our wired world.

Both Phakchok Rinpoche and Erric Solomon have the gift of using rich and humorous examples from their own lives to make their points. The net result: a user-friendly guide to understanding how to work with our mind.

Daniel Goleman and Tara Bennett-Goleman

INTRODUCING
RADICAL
HAPPINESS

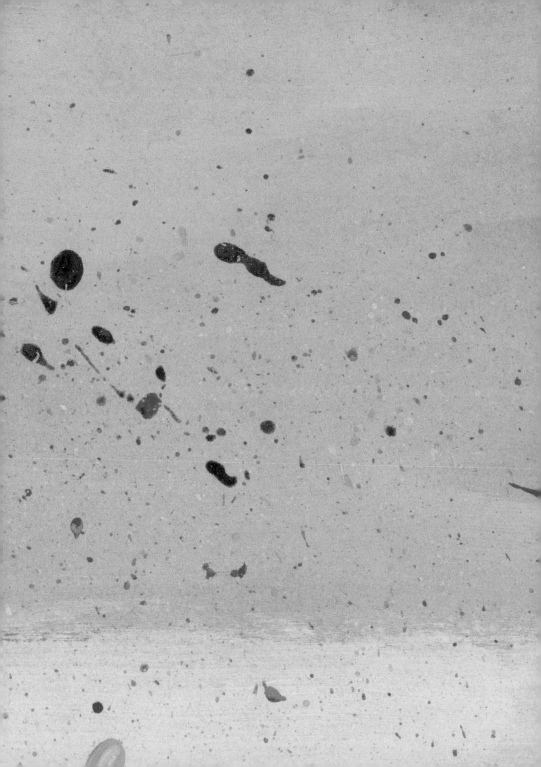

CHAPTER 1

Why you Need Radical Happiness, or How to Be Less of a Dog and More of a Lion

This book is about happiness.

Okay, we probably should stop right now, because we can hear what you're thinking. And yes, we know: Who needs another book on happiness? And on top of that, who needs another book on happiness from a couple of Buddhists? If the goal of Buddhism is to become completely enlightened, why do you need a book about a trivial, fleeting mood like happiness?

Well, we think we could *all* use a bit more happiness. And this book offers something different: a real path to happiness. We don't explore just one single solitary thing called happiness—as if it were a bronze statue in the town square—but the different kinds and the different dimensions of happiness, because happiness is a beautiful and many-splendored thing.

We *are* Buddhists, and it's true that Buddhism speaks mostly about enlightenment. But without a solid foundation of contentment, basic sanity, and a decent self-image, you can't flourish in life—either as a spiritual practitioner or as a practitioner of daily life. Not everyone wants to become a Buddhist, but doesn't everyone want to be able to flourish and enjoy what life has to offer? We all want to be able to cope, without losing our sh*t when things don't work out. And that last point is the heart of what radical happiness really is. It's a subtle sense of well-being we can always access, especially when things are not so great (as in, when they really suck).

How can we experience this kind of happiness? By making a slight but radical shift in the way we live our lives. The root of happiness is found not in specific circumstances; it's found in the way we relate to all of our experiences—including the chaos and confusion we might find ourselves in the middle of. So learning how *you* can shift, moment to moment, the way you relate to the world and to all the crazy stuff that runs through your mind—that is what this book is about. We'll also encourage you to have a few good laughs along the way, as you learn to make the shift.

What we offer here is a user's guide for your mind. (The mind is the most important device you have in your life, and nobody helps you figure out how to use it!) We will guide you through thought experiments, contemplation exercises, and meditation practices to help you get the most from your mind. This book also comes from a unique perspective: it is the result of a meeting of minds between a Silicon Valley entrepreneur and a Tibetan Buddhist guru. East meets West, ancient wisdom meets modern science, and what you end up with is a truly original perspective on how to actualize life's full potential.

Radical happiness is not theoretical. It's something we've tested on ourselves, our family, our friends, and the thousands of other people who have come to our workshops, retreats, and seminars. Like all good app developers, we did a lot of beta testing, made some big mistakes, and then worked on getting the bugs out. And that helped us figure out how to make the process of mastering our mind something everyone can do—and enjoy.

Oddly enough, our explorations and experimentation have taught us that happiness starts with *unhappiness*. So, let's start there. Let us introduce ourselves with some of our stories of unhappiness—how our struggles with anger and despondency led us to some important changes in our own lives.

DISCOVERING THE WISDOM OF A LION

· · · · · · · PHAKCHOK RINPOCHE · · · · · · ·

As a small child I was chosen, in a traditional Tibetan fashion, as an incarnation of a highly respected and powerful meditation teacher. Therefore, when I went to school in the monastery, my professors had big expectations for me. They put a lot of pressure on me to live up to the example of this great master from the past. But rather than rise to the occasion I, like many teenagers, rebelled against all the expectations and pressure. I just became more and more angry about everything and everyone. Behind my back, the other monks called me the "anger ball," and when I was in a bad mood everyone tried to get as far away from me as possible. It was no fun.

I thought, "just because you think I am an incarnation of some meditation teacher doesn't mean anything to me. I don't even know if I believe everything the Buddha says."

Even though I was studying lots of philosophy, which I found gratifying to my intellect (for it was like solving a difficult puzzle), I didn't seem to be getting a direct experience of the meaning of the great works I was studying. This only angered me more, and made me think I wasn't really much of a Buddhist, let alone that revered old meditator everyone said I was supposed to be. In fact, the only use I had for philosophy was that I got better and better at debate, and so I could easily defeat my peers, which gave me a great opportunity to channel my aggression toward other people. I guess beating them at debate was at least better than punching them out, which was a constant theme of my fantasies when I was seventeen.

Eventually, I couldn't keep it all bottled up anymore, so I went to my main meditation teacher, a great master named Nyoshul Khen Rinpoche, and told him how I felt. His response was to teach me a meditation practice on loving-kindness. He told me that every day I should strongly wish that everyone could be happy. And then, to take that further, imagine that everyone was becoming more and more happy. Not just one or two people, but *every single person*.

I practiced like that every day. And it seemed okay at first. My anger was subsiding. But then one day I asked myself, "Why do I need to wish for everybody's happiness if *they* don't really care about *me*? Why should I care about them, what's in it for me?"

This way of thinking only managed to irritate me even more. I also noticed that while my anger grew, any feelings of contentment and joy completely evaporated. I was becoming more and more miserable. I took a close look at myself and started comparing myself to my teacher. My parents and my teacher's generation were refugees who escaped Tibet and settled in exile in Nepal and India. They had to go through tremendous hardship leaving their homeland and adapting to a new country. My teacher particularly had to leave everything behind and spent most of his life in extreme poverty, lived very simply, and had very challenging health problems. I, on the other hand, had a nice place to live, plenty to eat, and many of the creature comforts of modern civilization. Yet, he was always radiating so much peace and joy that I loved to just sit in the same room as him. I figured it was worth speaking to him some more since not only did other people want to avoid me, I could barely stand being with myself.

I went to him and asked what I should do about my seemingly infinite capacity for anger and aggression.

His reply, "Stop behaving like a dog. Behave like a lion!"

"What does that mean?" I asked, "Should I roar? How will that improve my life and calm my mind?"

"When you throw a stone at a dog what does he do?" he asked.

"The dog chases the stone," I replied.

He said that was exactly what I was doing, acting like a dog—chasing each thought that came at me. I considered that for a moment. It was indeed true that when I had a first thought—for example, "That person pisses me off"—I would chase after it. Without even noticing, I would dwell on that thought, looping it over and over again, justifying it, coming up with all the reasons to be angry, and, in so doing, I would become the thought. Rinpoche pointed out to me how I was chasing after my angry thoughts, just like the dog chases after the stone.

"When you throw a stone at a lion," he continued, "the lion doesn't care about the stone at all. Instead, it immediately turns to see who is throwing the stone. Now think about it: if someone is throwing stones at a lion, what happens next when the lion turns to look?"

"The person throwing the stone either runs away or gets eaten," I said.

"Right you are," said my teacher. "Either way, no more stones!"

. . . .

This lesson is at the heart of this book. The point here is for you to learn how to refrain from habitually chasing every thought that comes through your head. By engaging in the exercises presented in the coming pages, you will become familiar with just being present, undisturbed by any thoughts and emotions that may arise. Furthermore, by wholeheartedly considering the welfare of others, your own mind will be more content, and it will be easier to be fully present. One supports the other.

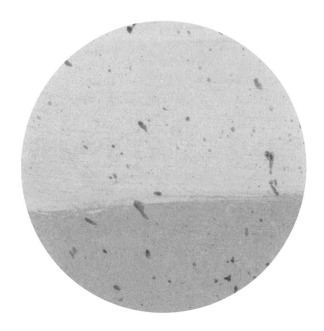

DESPERATE BUSINESSMAN

· · · · · · · · · E R R I C   S O L O M O N · · · · · · · ·

I was standing in the swimming pool at my beautiful house, and the view was fantastic. You could see the San Francisco skyline and two bridges reaching across the pristine blue of the bay to the north, and to the south, the northern edge of Silicon Valley. Hawks floated gracefully in the cloudless sky above, seeking rodents for nourishment. My wife gazed at me from the pool's edge, eyes filled with concern.

I wasn't swimming or moving at all. I was just standing there completely lost in the thoughts that were stuck in my head. I felt immune to my surroundings. For a moment, I snapped out of it and realized where I was. "I can't feel or enjoy anything," I said to Eva. "Not this perfectly warm, solar-heated pool, the amazing view, or… " My voice trailed off, as I somehow had the presence of mind not to say "my beautiful wife." "Or anything else." I continued, "I am totally numb."

I was vice president of software engineering at a successful tech company that had recently released really, really bad news during the quarterly call with Wall Street analysts. The stock tanked, then tanked some more. Almost all of our net worth, comfortably in seven figures, just went bye-bye. Instead of security, suddenly I was looking at a monster mortgage and about enough money in the bank to cover two months of expenses. How could I have been so stupid? I had it all, and now I would probably lose it all.

It's hard to empathize with an affluent guy who, through his own stupidity, just lost more money than most of us will ever have in the bank and who can't enjoy his swimming pool. But this just shows how, much of the time, suffering is the result of how we view things. And in this case, my narcissistic wallow was in complete control.

I left the pool, had a couple of stiff drinks, and went straight to bed. At 5:00 a.m. the phone rang. I dragged the receiver to my ear and said something vaguely resembling a *hello* into the mouthpiece. It was one of my main meditation teachers with whom I had been studying over the last twenty years or so. He was in France, leading his yearly summer meditation program.

He bellowed across the nine time zones that lay between us, "I am on the veranda with a glass of champagne celebrating impermanence," followed by the hearty sound of his boisterous laugh. I didn't have the presence of mind to notice, but it was pretty unlikely he was drinking champagne, let alone at 2:00 in the afternoon.

Bewildered (how did he know to call me?), I replied, "It's 5:00 a.m." as if he didn't know.

"Right now everything is fine. Don't think too much about yourself," he said and then hung up the phone. My feelings at that moment were an odd mix of appreciating the loving motivation of his phone call and kind of being ticked off that he woke me up to tell me not to think too much. I peeled myself out of bed, did my morning meditation, and got ready for work. As I stepped in the shower I reflected on the last few days of mental torture. There were two times I was kind of okay: when I was meditating (i.e., being completely in the "right now"), and when I was guiding my staff through this difficult time. Most people at work were going through something similar. We all just saw our stock options go to nothing. Some people had to rethink how to pay for their kids' college tuition, and others were wondering how they would pay off big consumer debts they'd accumulated when they thought they would have a hefty nest egg forever. At least I had a Silicon Valley VP's salary to fall back upon. Most of the team was in a financial bind they were not prepared for.

I was the department head, and people needed reassurance and a shoulder to cry on. So, during the ten-plus hours I was at work each day, there were a few moments I wasn't able to dwell on my own predicament (i.e., "think too much about myself") because it was my duty to respond to the needs of others. That teacher of mine always had an uncanny talent for catching me off guard and doing something a little unconventional that I wouldn't always grasp the meaning of at first but that I would appreciate later. To this day, I thank him for that crazy little call that snapped me out of it.

· · · · · · · · · · ·

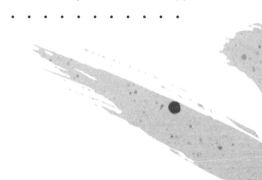

FROM UNHAPPINESS TO HAPPINESS

What do these stories have in common? In each case, our problem could be resolved by being more present-moment focused and by thinking of the welfare of others. Could the path to happiness really be that simple? Well, it's easy *to say* but a bit more challenging to actually *do*. But pulling off those two things is the very basis of radical happiness—of real, sustained happiness.

When we become familiar with remaining in the present moment, and during moments of kindness and compassion, radical happiness emerges naturally. This doesn't mean that we are in a blissed-out state of denial about all the crap in our lives—radically happy people experience sadness, and disappointment. But those feelings don't overwhelm the subtle sense of well-being that permeates the mind of a radically happy person.

So what do we have to do to learn to be radically happy?

In the first part of this book we look at how to transform our relationship to ourselves by changing how we relate to thoughts and emotions and learning to be more present-moment focused. We call this *basic happiness*. What makes basic happiness a radical change is that we become less like a dog chasing stones: habitually running down thoughts and emotions and looping them over and over again and again even when we don't want to. We can learn to do this by spending a little time practicing remaining present each day; we call this *meditation*. But we shouldn't just leave the present moment behind when we leave our meditation session. So we will explain how to integrate a present-moment focus into everything we do, all day long.

In the second part we look at how we relate to the world around us, especially the people around us. Through contemplative reflection, we gradually begin to understand the common bond of experience we all share. This leads to empathy as we interact with others and learn to act more considerately—even with people who really, really annoy us. When our actions are informed by considering others' needs, the result is *interconnected happiness*—a special sense of satisfaction and joy. There is a counterintuitive switcheroo here: We usually think that to properly take care of ourselves and our loved ones, we have to put our needs and theirs before all others. But interconnected happiness arises through cultivating loving-kindness and compassion and by learning to value others in almost the same way we value ourselves. We'll see how that works.

Everyone is familiar with the Golden Rule—"Do unto others as you would have them do unto you"—and many of us have heard some of the emerging science on the benefits of compassion. Yet none of those things tell us *how* to make it happen in our lives. Not only will we show you how to get there step-by-step, but we will also show you how to do it in a way that seemlessly fits into the life you are already living. That way you can easily try it out and see for yourself how interconnected happiness really functions.

In the third part we look at how these first two kinds of happiness reinforce each other, leading to radical happiness. When we are in the present-moment experience of basic happiness, we are no longer distracted by involuntarily chasing our thoughts. Through cultivating a consistent attention to the needs of others, which forms the basis of interconnected happiness, we appreciate and begin to live in accord with the natural interdependence between ourselves, our world, and all its inhabitants.

We need the strength of meditation's mindful awareness to stabilize love and compassion so that they begin to arise naturally in every situation, even when other people are acting really badly. When we think of others, we forget about ourselves. This allows the almost constant, habitual, doglike chasing of thoughts and emotions to fall away. At the moment when thoughts for others' well-being fill our mind, our normal self-centered way of thinking has completely dissolved. Then, if we have been training ourselves in being present, we can experience ourselves and the world around us in a radically different way—unhindered by our usual habitual patterns of thoughts and emotions. That way of being is the essence of radical happiness. We will include some science, some thought experiments, and a bunch of easy-to-do meditation exercises you can try out for yourself and integrate into your daily routine.

Learning to be radically happy should lead to an all-pervasive sense of contentment, or at the very least help you welcome more joy in your life—you know, to have more fun more of the time. Meditation doesn't have to be boring. Caring for others' needs doesn't have to be a chore.

Most importantly, the book not only is a guide for *how* to be radically happy, but it is also a guide to understanding *why* these exercises and principles work. That way, radical happiness becomes something that makes sense, something you can test out and experience. You don't have to just take the word of two authors, no matter how sensitive, good-looking, and intelligent they may be. You can figure it out for yourself.

As you read, you'll hear us use the word *we* a lot. Most of the time it means all of us: readers, authors, and everybody else. This is because radical happiness isn't an endpoint that "we," the authors, have reached but a continuous process, a way of engaging life. It is something each of us can learn, participate in, sometimes struggle with, and always laugh about. It's like playing a musical instrument. Even someone who is a master concert pianist will tell you that there are still new things to learn every day about the piano. We, the authors, may have been practicing the radical happiness instrument a little longer than you, but all of us are still just practitioners. If you practice the guitar a little bit every day, you probably won't be able to play like Jerry Garcia, Jack White, Joan Jett, or Bonnie Raitt, but after a little while you will be able to play enough to give yourself and your friends a lot of pleasure. It's the same with practicing radical happiness. By practicing what's in this book, after a little while you'll be able to enjoy the result. And so will the people around you.

Let's get started. First things first: we need to begin with our unhappiness, and look at precisely how we *usually* go about trying to find happiness. And we need to ask, how well is that working out?

CHAPTER 2

The Looking -for- Happiness Conundrum

magine for a moment that you're waking up in a hospital bed, looking at the ceiling, bathed in fluorescent light. Your brain is foggy, and you can't quite recall what happened. After a few long minutes a doctor comes in and lets you know that you were hit by a car while standing on a street corner. She also lets you know, hesitantly, you have permanently lost the use of your legs and will spend the rest of your life in a wheelchair.

How do you feel? On a one-to-ten scale, how happy do you think you'd be hearing that news? How happy do you think you'd be a year later?

Now imagine another scenario. Your partner bursts into the room, waking you from a delicious sleep. She is so excited, your first thought is that maybe she has completely taken leave of her senses. As you sit upright in the bed, you realize that those are not the movements of someone who has lost her marbles but of ecstatic joy. Suddenly the peals of joyful noise begin to make sense, and you realize that the lottery ticket you had forgotten about is worth money. A lot of money—$150 million to be precise—which is way more than you'd ever dared to dream was possible.

How do you feel? Perhaps you find yourself joining your partner, dancing around the room making the same movements that only a moment ago led you to consider that maybe she had gone off the deep end. So, you're pretty happy, right? A ten on the one-to-ten scale, maybe? How about a year into it? Still happy?

What do you think? Happier in a wheelchair or with all that money? Most people say the answer to this question is blindingly obvious: it's the money. However, somewhat counterintuitively, this turns out not to be true. There is good research supporting a different conclusion.

In 1978, a study compared the level of happiness of twenty-nine paraplegics and twenty-two lottery winners. Initially, researchers reported an improvement in the overall feeling of happiness for the lottery winners and a proportional diminishment of happiness for the paraplegics. However, *after only one year*, the level of happiness in these two groups returned to pre-event levels. In other words, there was no discernible difference in the level of happiness between these two groups, despite the extreme differences in external circumstances![1] Go figure. But the truth is, we really suck when it comes to predicting what will make us happy.

LET'S MAKE ONE THING VERY CLEAR

We're going to go on a little trip, a short vacation you might say, to examine our relationship with happiness. But we might as well tell you right off the bat, there is one thing we very much believe to be true: **real happiness—what we call radical happiness—is not found in situations and things.** It takes awhile for that simple truth to really sink in, because we spend so much time trying to disprove it, even though we know it in our hearts. So, we will repeat:

RADICAL HAPPINESS
IS NOT
FOUND
IN
SITUATIONS
AND THINGS.

Lots of people hear that and say, "Duh! Of course happiness can't be found in material possessions or by simply creating the right circumstances. If you've read a Hallmark greeting card, you know that." But if we take a careful look, with an inquisitive mind, at how we actually spend our time, it will reveal that secretly most of us behave as if we do really believe that circumstances and things *are* the key to happiness.

And that is a conundrum: what we know to be true and how we're behaving are out of sync. Some investigation is called for. In order to make a slight but radical shift in our life, we need to look closely at how we usually go about finding happiness and see what the issues are. And we need to really test our hypothesis: we won't find happiness in situations and things, but we behave as if we will, day in, day out, most of the time.

HAPPINESS IS RIGHT AROUND THE CORNER, THE NEXT THING WILL DO THE TRICK

Everyone wants to know the secret to happiness and to having a meaningful life. At first, it might seem obvious that we ought to be able to find meaning and satisfaction by *creating the right circumstances*: a nice place to live; an interesting, well-paying job; a satisfying marriage; happy, successful children; many loving friends; and perhaps an exotic vacation from time to time. And yet, even if we are among the few who achieve *all* of these wonderful circumstances, do you think our "success" would offer us any more than a brief respite from our anxieties, frustrations, and dissatisfactions?

If we were watching a movie of our lives, including the internal dialogue going on in our mind, it would be clear to us that down deep we believe it's impossible to find happiness except by repeating an endless cycle that looks something like this:

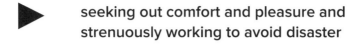

▶ seeking out comfort and pleasure and strenuously working to avoid disaster

▶❚❚ getting some temporary relief or none at all

⮌ starting to seek comfort again

It is another conundrum: We work so hard to create pleasurable circumstances, so that if and when we finally achieve them, everything will be okay. Yet, almost as soon as we get there we are already worrying about how to keep it going, or we are working toward another set of pleasure-giving or pain-avoiding goals. In spite of all our efforts we can't shake an underlying insecurity that this entire strategy will never really work.

When our carefully laid plans for a comfy, cozy, permanently cushy existence fail to work out—we get sick, run out of money, get into a big argument—what do we do? Does such failure to find happiness this time around mean that life's promise will remain unfulfilled unless we can somehow wrestle things back into something positive?

It makes perfectly good sense, of course, to spend time working to improve the conditions of our lives. Certainly, there is nothing wrong with taking good care of ourselves and those we love. But it makes very little sense to do the same things over and over again—things that don't produce lasting happiness—while expecting a different, more satisfying result.

For example, the satisfaction of a good meal fades pretty quickly after it is consumed—or it can even fade during the meal itself, if we get carried away and stuff ourselves. Friends and lovers come and go, and, even in the best conditions, our nearest and dearest can bore, irritate, or anger us from time to time. Although you love your parents, perhaps living with them drove you nuts and you couldn't wait to get your own place; but then, after getting set up on your own, you began to miss them. If we're fortunate enough to enjoy professional success, we may at first become thrilled and feel as if everything is finally right in the universe. Our ship has come in. We are captains of our fate at last. But, too soon another of life's challenges falls upon us and it's hard to recall any of those good feelings. Undeterred, we persevere, tirelessly and confidently working to establish the next happy circumstance, which, in turn, rapidly fades just like the rest of them.

What's the problem here? To put it very simply: **circumstances are, by their very nature, fleeting and unstable.** How, then, can any of us possibly expect to make a foundation for lasting contentment and meaning from such transience and instability? This is one aspect of the looking-for-happiness conundrum: we act as if happiness will be found in pleasing circumstances, and yet circumstances by their very nature are temporary and are thus bound eventually to disappoint us.

There must be another, better, more fruitful way to go about fulfilling our desire to find happiness and meaning in life. What might it be?

If we want to properly answer this question, we need to keep digging into and examining the typical methods we use to seek happiness to see if there might be some others that would really work.

DO WE REALLY KNOW WHAT WILL MAKE US HAPPY?

Remember at the beginning of the chapter how obvious it seemed that you would be much happier as a lottery winner than stuck in a wheelchair? Even when presented with evidence contrary to our assumptions, there is still a stubborn part of us that doesn't want to believe it. This just shows how bad we are at predicting how circumstances will actually affect our degree of contentment.

To take one example, friends of ours, a couple named Jim and Sam, after many years of scrimping and saving, were finally able to buy a live-work loft in an up-and-coming part of the city. They were totally stoked that they would be able to have a place they could both live in and run their consulting business out of. They could roll out of bed, get some coffee, and get online. Plus, the neighborhood had a bunch of inexpensive restaurants and good night life. Before this magnificent purchase, they were free to take only work that interested them. But, after having located and purchased the loft of their dreams, they found themselves struggling to make the mortgage payments. As a result, they felt constrained to take on contracts they wouldn't even have considered in the past. In constant worry about meeting deadlines and finding new clients, and their constant negotiations with the other co-op owner in the building about maintenance issues, they found themselves much less happy than anticipated. Their loft was as much a prison as a refuge.

Then the 2008 financial crisis erupted, and high-paying clients grew scarce. Jim and Sam saw their mortgage turned upside down: their loft was worth less than they paid for it, but they were stuck with it because they couldn't afford to sell it—they wouldn't end up with enough money to settle their debts. In the end, after many years, new clients did come along and the real-estate market improved, but their pursuit of their hopes and dreams caused them to endure a stressful, heart-wrenching existence for years. Happiness and satisfaction eluded them. There were some good times and great parties in the loft, for sure, but the price of these transient moments of satisfaction was ongoing stress, worry, and sacrifice. It was far from the TV-commercial version of what the dream home will do for you. And, to be sure, our friends are not alone in seeking happiness in the perfect shelter only to find themselves living in a painful trap. How could such smart people guess so wrong about what would make them happy?

There is, in fact, a growing body of scientific evidence that our predictions about what will make us happy or unhappy are often just plain wrong. For example, a recent study found that professors who were up for tenure believed they would be very unhappy if denied it.[2] Yet, when researchers later compared the happiness of the professors who eventually received tenure with those who did not, they found no meaningful difference.

You may be wondering, if we are so bad at predicting what will make us happy, why don't we notice and learn from our mistakes? Well, scientists have been wondering the same thing, and it looks like not only are we bad at making happiness predictions, we also seem to be very bad at *remembering* what we thought would make us happy or unhappy after the fact. In other words, we forget or minimize our bad predictions.

For example, one study focused on voters in the Obama-McCain 2008 presidential race.[3] The researchers found that before the election, McCain voters anticipated being extremely unhappy in the event of an Obama win. Many of them said it would be not just a catastrophe for the country but an almost unbearable burden for them personally. A week after the election, however, these same voters reported themselves much less unhappy than predicted. But here's the interesting part: They also tended *not* to remember their earlier prediction of how bad it was all going to be. Or, if they did remember it, they minimized its intensity.

All of this seems to suggest that not only are we unskilled at making predictions about what will make us happy or unhappy, but we also don't even seem to learn from past prediction failures, for the simple reason that we don't remember them very well. Driven forward in this state of amnesia, we continue to plan actions based on the same kinds of flawed predictions, exaggerating or underestimating how good or bad this or that action will make us feel. Although we endlessly engage in all kinds of frenzied activities in search of happiness, they rarely give us the sort of satisfaction we seek. In fact, instead of happiness, these very activities more often than not bring us more difficulties.

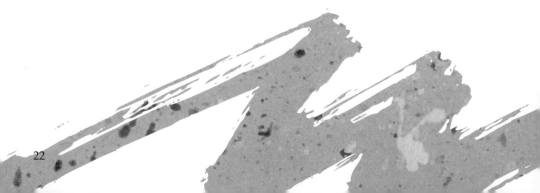

SEEKING HAPPINESS IN CIRCUMSTANCES
ONLY LEADS TO FUTURE DISSATISFACTION

What the looking-for-happiness conundrum comes down to is this: **in seeking happiness we can easily end up with even more frustration and dissatisfaction.** Even when we manage to achieve a degree of happiness, it's temporary and tends to dissipate rapidly. That's not the end of it, however: such temporary victories over discontent not only fade quickly but also actually create the very basis for further rounds of discomfort and dissatisfaction.

Let's try a little thought experiment. Let's assume that while reading this book you've chosen to sit in your favorite comfortable chair. Perhaps the window is open, there's a nice breeze, your feet are up, you're absorbed by the book, and all seems right with the world. It can be quite a treat to be sitting comfortably, good book in hand, don't you think?

But, if you were told you weren't allowed to move from this incredibly comfortable position for the next ten hours, how long would it take before the position became very uncomfortable? Probably almost immediately. What seemed so blissfully cozy and comfy only moments earlier has now become a source of discomfort, even pain!

Of course, even without a command to remain motionless, we'd soon find our original posture uncomfortable in some way. So we'd start to fidget and shift—recross our legs, adjust a cushion, close the window. (We might even think how nice it would be to have a drink or a snack or maybe put on some music.) Although we normally don't look at it this way, the truth seems to be this: **our future discomfort is generated the moment we settle into a comfortable position.**

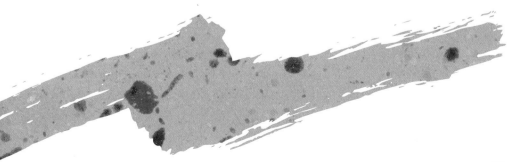

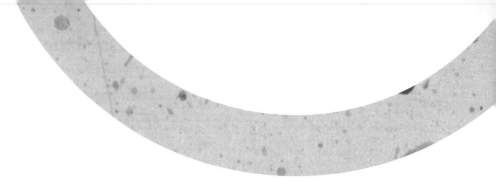

IN FACT, DO WE EVEN KNOW HOW TO ENJOY OURSELVES?

Nobody is suggesting we shouldn't try to relax and enjoy life. That's not the point. Relaxation and enjoyment that are not in themselves the problem. No, the problem is this: **the way we usually go about securing happiness doesn't really work.** Even when finding ourselves blessed with an abundance of truly pleasant circumstances, do we really know how to fully enjoy them?

Recall for a moment the last truly great day you had. What was it that made the day so wonderful? Was it the location? Your companions? Activities? Perhaps all of these.

· · · · · · · · · ERRIC SOLOMON · · · · · · · ·

Every year my wife, Eva, and I would go to Cabo San Lucas in February to escape the relentless winter rain. It was only a two-hour flight from Silicon Valley, and we would leave in the morning and be on a stunning beach the same afternoon. One trip, we were having an especially idyllic time. We would start every morning meditating while looking out on the ocean, and then go for a swim. Sitting on our beach chairs we were in bliss. I put my arm out and lovingly drew beautiful, dear Eva toward me and then I heard myself gently say with a little sigh: "Too bad every day can't be like this." As soon as I heard these words slip off of my tongue, I realized that even during this perfect moment, I was subtly dissatisfied.

· · · · · · · · · ·

During such wonderful times, haven't we all caught ourselves thinking, "Too bad every day can't be like this?" Even when things are going splendidly we can't fully enjoy ourselves because instead we're thinking, "Too bad…" At such a point we might find ourselves thinking about what we can do to extend the moment or, if this proves impossible, to repeat it. Either that or we are recording everything, snapping pictures and filming videos, trying to capture the wonderful moment. It's not hard to see how the enjoyment has been overshadowed by the attempts to extend, repeat, or capture it. Instead of relaxing enjoyably, you are busily thinking and scheming and documenting. How desperate.

Even during very pleasurable circumstances, it seems, our experience cannot help but be colored by that slight underlying restlessness that anticipates an end to the good times. Everyone is familiar with the Sunday afternoon blues, even after a perfect weekend. This regret, this subtle sense of dissatisfaction, comes from our understanding—explicit or not—that this moment is already slipping into the past. Even the happiness of the present moment is overshadowed as we make plans to avoid the next possible moment of unhappiness.

Is this any way to enjoy good times?

So, what if we could make the day last? Wouldn't that solve our problem? For example, maybe our perfect day was spent on the beach with our besties. Imagine for a moment that we could just lock it in so that every day from now on would be a beach day with our favorite gang, the sun always shining, for years without end. How do you think this would turn out? Would we run out of things to talk about? Yearn for a different beach? Or an occasional rainy day, just for contrast? Or new kinds of food? New friends? Most likely—as we all know if we think about it—after a while we would get tired of the sand and sun, tired of the same friends and food, and we'd grow bored. The same external circumstances that seemed to be producing such happiness and contentment become—inescapably—the foundation for future dissatisfaction.

The lesson here? Looking for happiness in situations, circumstances, and things has three main problems:

1.

We aren't very good at predicting
what will make us happy.

2.

If and when we do seem to get it right, and we do
manage to create all the right circumstances for
happiness, we nonetheless find it's difficult for us to
fully enjoy them. Either we become preoccupied with
prolonging them, or unhappy at their fleeting nature.

3.

What first makes us happy becomes in turn
the very basis for future discontent.

The conundrum is that the way we act—spending so much time seeking happiness in circumstances—is out of accord with how we actually find happiness. In fact, recent research seems to support the idea that circumstances actually contribute roughly only 10 percent of our overall sense of satisfaction and contentment in life.[4]

Following the tradition I was born into, I was a monk right up until I got married. I had a very romantic idea about what marriage was, and my expectations were quite high. I loved everything about my wife. She was extraordinarily kind and warmhearted, intelligent, and well-educated, and I loved looking at her. I was utterly convinced that being married to her would be a constant source of joy.

Sometime before getting married, my father very sweetly gave me his advice for marital harmony: when your wife gets upset with you, don't get angry, don't talk back, just listen, and when you get tired of listening, just get up and quietly walk away.

My father's advice might sound a little naive from a modern perspective. My father came from a nomadic region of eastern Tibet, and women were not always treated as equals; yet my grandfather's side of the family had several spiritually accomplished women renowned for their wisdom. And it was my mother who was instrumental in raising me and my younger brother and two younger sisters. She was not only a remarkable mother but a wonderful life partner to my father who helped him in materializing all his aspirations. It was important to my parents that their children were raised to cherish the capability and capacity of everyone, no matter their gender (or background). So it was in this spirit of respect and equality that my father offered his advice.

During the first few weeks of our marriage, everything seemed perfect. Although we had spent time together before we were married, now we were together 24-7 and it was great. I loved our time together, and found our values were even more in line than I imagined. Our time together was so blissful, I didn't want anything to change.

But that was the problem. Before marriage, each of us was used to living our own independent lives. After a few weeks of living together and accommodating the new lifestyle, things slowly started to unwind. It started very subtly at first with small quarrels, but later the quarrels became part of our daily routine. And I was trying to control everything.

At first my wife was trying to accommodate as much as possible and trying to hold it together, but one day during one of the quarrels, I remembered my father's advice. I tried to listen patiently for a while, but then I started to think, "Why does she insist on ruining things like this? Doesn't she see how good things were, just the way they were?" So I got up and began to quietly walk away.

"Where do you think you are going? We haven't finished our conversation, yet!" she exclaimed. She had been educated in the West and wasn't going to stand for my backward, autocratic behavior.

I was so shocked. I had no idea marriage was going to be so difficult. In the months leading up to our marriage I could only imagine my idealized version of marriage and the happiness it would bring. Confronted by this new reality, I ran out of the room.

I had a lot to learn about marriage, let alone finding happiness.

· · · · · · · · · · ·

If lasting contentment can't be found in circumstances, where might it be found? What other options might there be beyond our preoccupation with how our situations could be improved, or prolonged, or avoided?

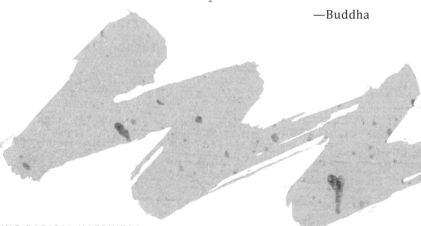

Do not think about the past,
nor start thinking about the future,
but leave the mind in the
present moment.

—Buddha

WHERE, OH WHERE, DO WE LOOK TO BE HAPPY?

In 2010, a study of what causes us to be happy determined that people are happiest when they are completely absorbed in the present moment, rather than caught up in wandering thoughts.[5] In this study, the researchers Mathew Killingsworth and Daniel Gilbert found that nearly half the time we are lost in distraction. Not only that, but during those periods of distraction time-study participants were less happy than when they were fully engaged in the present moment. The study identified distraction as "mind-wandering"—a state of being completely distracted from the present moment by thinking about thoughts. In fact, in the study the authors said that mind-wandering (or rather, the lack thereof) is an excellent predictor of happiness.

One surprising finding of this study was that even when we find ourselves forced to engage in a distasteful task, on average we're much happier than when we're lost in mind-wandering. For example, the study found that people stuck in a bad traffic jam are substantially happier when their minds are focused on the present moment rather than when they are daydreaming. This was even true when compared with the subset of mind-wanderers who were daydreaming about something they really enjoyed!

Think about this for a moment. We are happier stuck in horrible traffic, looking at the hopelessly long line of slow-moving cars in front of us, than if we allow our minds to wander to someplace far more pleasant. This is more than surprising! The science, in fact, supports the following nonintuitive assertion: situating oneself firmly and mindfully in what is present—no matter what it is—is intimately connected to genuine happiness.

Isn't that a fairly radical thing to consider?

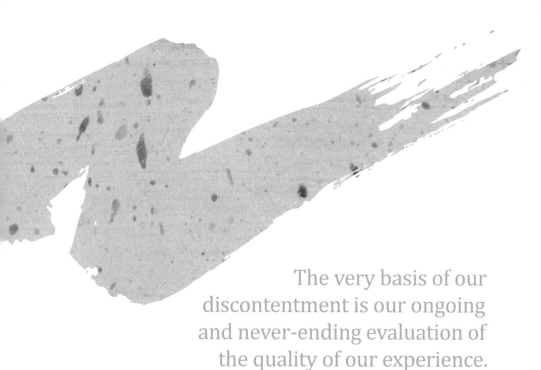

The very basis of our
discentment is our ongoing
and never-ending evaluation of
the quality of our experience.

—Tulku Urgyen Rinpoche

**IF THIS IS TRUE, THEN WHAT IS IT THAT KEEPS US
FROM JUST BEING IN THE PRESENT MOMENT?**

If you listen carefully to your own mind, you'll quickly notice that
you're continuously caught up in a conversation with yourself about
what you're experiencing. It's like having a perpetual inner sports
announcer, describing and evaluating the plays as they arise in your
day-to-day activities. This color commentary we all partake in reports
to us our current successes and failures. It offers statistics and metrics,
so we can know where we stand, whether we're winning or losing, and
by how much. Truth is, we don't even feel we're really experiencing
anything unless it is mediated back to us via this commentary. We
endlessly describe, measure, assess, and evaluate everything that
happens to us. In nearly every moment, we make judgment after
judgment as to how well or badly things are going for us, and then we

engage in thinking about what we just thought about and evaluate *that*. Each thought simply leads to the next and then the next, until some new input from one of our senses interrupts this and the process starts all over again.

For example, we might notice as we're leaving our apartment that one of our neighbors is whizzing by in her brand-new car. In no time at all, the thought strikes us that it's well past time we bought *ourselves* a new car. Effortlessly, thoughts and visualizations and plans describing our path to our own new car present themselves to us. "Hmmm. I'll need a substantial raise, which I deserve! But they'll never give it to me. Maybe what I really need to think about is finding a new job, one where they appreciate me more. Let's face it: I've got a dead-end job and I'll never get paid what I'm worth there. Hey! It might even be fun to have a new challenge. I'm so fed up with my idiotic coworkers, anyway." And then, as we drift further and further into thinking about how we're currently being ripped off by our ungrateful employers, as we amble along ever more deeply into thoughts about our job prospects, the wind stiffens a bit and we think, "Ohmigod, it's gotten so much chillier. Before I head into my hellhole of a job, I better find a sweater. I wonder where that blue one is? Is it back from the cleaners yet? Did he forget to pick up the dry cleaning again? Jeez. No matter how often I remind him, he's always forgetting to do what he's said he'll do. This really gets on my nerves. It is so annoying! Yeah, maybe it's time for THE BIG TALK." We're off to the races once more, and all of that happened in the time it took to walk to the curb and back.

It's our habit to constantly measure our experience and then think about it. And, if it turns out the way we like, we immediately start to think about how to maintain the obvious goodness. But, as we noted above, hidden right within our wish to cling to what's pleasing us is a subtle dissatisfaction with the whole thing. Why is this? **It's because we cannot help but already be engaged in subtle anticipation of or worry about coming change and possible loss.**

In the same way, if it turns out we don't like our present situation, we begin right away to think about ways to get ourselves out of what we don't like. Not only do we have the dissatisfaction that comes along with any unpleasant experience, but we have the fear or concern that we may have to endure this unpleasant experience for a longer, perhaps unbearable, period of time.

> I've been through lots of terrible things in my life. Some of them happened.
>
> —Mark Twain

Normally, when we encounter someone wandering down the sidewalk talking to himself, we figure the person is at least a bit weird and possibly suffering from mental illness. Yet, if we're honest with ourselves, we can see that most of the time we're fully engaged in nonstop, if silent, inner conversation, and, were we to speak all of this aloud, it would likely cause those within earshot to question our own sanity. And not simply because of our deviation from social norms. No, that's not it. The reason others would question the soundness of our mind is that so much of our internal monologue is just so silly, trivial, and oddly self-obsessed.

Of course, some of what we think about is important—problems that need solving, plans that have to be sorted, tasks to prioritize—but our habit of constantly evaluating the quality of experience into likes and dislikes and things we want to create or avoid is all-consuming and out of control. We do it constantly, and yet most of it is useless.

It's not like we're actually solving important problems and making meaningful life decisions every time we wait for our friends to show up for lunch. Imagine instead that we could actually be so present and stable in the moment that we could choose to allow our mind to wander, because it suits our needs.[6] Not only would we be happier, but it would be a lot less exhausting!

Most of us already have had a handful of instances when we arrived fully in the present moment and, once there, found ourselves suddenly free from the constant judgment, comparison, and evaluation that usually characterizes our experience.

This moment of complete presence can happen during moments of intense physical exercise or play. We have a friend, for example, who loves kitesurfing. The sport is so dangerous that he has no choice but to concentrate completely on what he's doing. He says that when he's in such a *zone of focus* his normal thinking mind drops away and he finds himself completely immersed in the moment and its flow-state.

In the Killingsworth and Gilbert study mentioned above, it turned out that people were most likely to be in the present moment not while doing something dangerous but while having sex. What a surprise! But, in fact, it needn't be danger or sex. People in other studies report complete *presence in the moment* during peak physical performance in sports, computer programming, playing improvised music, or even while being absorbed in video games. When they talk about such experiences, they report being completely engrossed in the activity and free from ordinary thoughts or concerns.[7]

What do all of these activities have in common? At these kinds of moments, we're so fully integrated in the present moment that habitual measuring and evaluation of the quality of experience is interrupted or suspended. Is the good news here, then, that all we need to do is immerse ourselves in lovemaking, or an improvisational music-making jam, or endless hours with eyes glued to a computer screen while hacking out some code?

If that's the case, we still have a problem—and a big one.

We are still hooking our happiness to specific sets of external (and thus ever-changing) circumstances over which we can have no real control. We're still doomed to be the victims of these always-shifting circumstances.

Why worry?
If you can do something, do it.
If not, how can worrying help?
—Shantideva

BEGIN BY PLACING YOUR ATTENTION
ON THE PRESENT MOMENT

When things aren't going our way and there is something we can do, then we should do it. But we should do it without wasting time worrying about what happens if it doesn't work. Or, if nothing can be done, isn't worrying only going to make it worse? And if things are going well, then why not just be completely present in the enjoyment of it instead of getting distracted by thoughts of prolonging and maintaining or regretting that it will soon be over? The more we place our attention in the present moment rather than focusing on what might happen or thinking about what has happened, the more we can enjoy life's great moments. Furthermore, the more we keep our attention on what is happening now, the less we will exaggerate and allow the bad times to overwhelm us.

In order to find real, radical happiness we need methods to help us establish contentment and meaning in life whether things are going our way or not. As long as we're looking for happiness in circumstances, we'll waste a great deal of our energy hoping for the good and fearing the bad.

Instead of being stuck on this seesaw, we can free ourselves from the ups and downs of hope and fear by relearning where to put our attention. Instead of wandering wherever our thoughts take us, chasing one thought after another and another, we can retrain our attention to remain more and more in the present moment. That way, when good things happen, we'll be better able to enjoy them, and when disaster strikes, we can still be okay.

How do we do this? The very first step is to learn how to gain more control over our ever-evaluating minds by making a slight yet profoundly radical shift in the way we place our attention. This is the beginning of experiencing happiness, and the best way to accomplish this turns out to be meditation.

The kind of meditation explained in this book has been taught and practiced and tested for thousands of years. It involves attention-training exercises that provide optimal ways to learn to bring the mind out of its habitual pattern of thinking about thoughts and into the present moment.

Remember the example of the lion and the dog? Being like a dog means that, like a dog chasing stones, we become lost in thinking about thoughts—chasing one thought with another in a seemingly endless chain. Being like a lion means that instead of looking at each stone, we turn our attention to the stone thrower—in our case that means the mind itself. By coming to know your mind and how you can master it, you can discover a subtle sense of well-being that can't be shaken no matter what happens.

So, let's take a little break from the fast lane, shall we?

CHAPTER 3

The Indispensable Basis of Happiness: Getting to Know Your Mind

How many times have you thoroughly enjoyed a movie only to find out that a friend hated it? The movie itself is neither inherently great nor awful. We create a lot of consensus with others about what we like in movies, of course, but ultimately the experience of movie goodness or badness resides in the mind of the viewer. This is true not only for movies but for whatever happens: the final arbiter of experience—of joy and sorrow, entertaining and boring, good and bad—is the mind.

· · · · · · · · · E R R I C   S O L O M O N · · · · · · · · ·

On a good day, my daily trek down the San Francisco peninsula to my job in Mountain View in Silicon Valley took forty-five minutes.

But there weren't many good days.

I was traveling in a pack of pretty aggressive drivers, so quite often one of these drivers would try to get ahead by weaving back and forth across lanes. And more often than not Mr. Lane Weaver would swerve in front of me, passing within a foot of my bumper, causing me to abruptly hit the brakes. I would get so enraged that I would then weave through the traffic myself— doing the very exact thing that I was so righteously indignant about—just so I could pass Mr. Lane Weaver and cut in front of *him*. I gave him what he deserved. If it was a really bad day, I might even slow down a little once I got in front of old Mr. Weaver. I might give Weaver a look or a certain kind of hand gesture. Take that, bastard!

Some days I would carpool with a friend. During one of these days when I was a passenger, my friend was excitedly explaining some new code he was working on when suddenly, someone snaking through the traffic careened into our lane, a little too close for comfort. My friend lightly tapped the brake. I was about to commiserate with him about what a jerk that driver was, so we could do some war whooping together, but he didn't seem to notice anything unusual at all. He continued driving with the same expression of excitement and kept talking about the cool new algorithm he was working on.

It seems like the same event: Someone cuts us off on the road. *Yet, the experience of it is vastly different from person to person*. I would get really upset, but my friend didn't seem to think much about it at all, just gently pressing his foot on the brake.

He didn't know it, but when I saw his detached response, I felt embarrassed by how I behaved while driving. My getting all worked up isn't going to change the situation or end aggressive driving. It's just going to turn me into a jerk.

• • • • • • • • • • •

While circumstances contribute to what we experience, it is the mind that determines *the quality* of our experience, how our experience affects our overall well-being. Since our mind determines how we experience things, if we want to experience basic happiness we need to work with our mind—the ultimate shaper of all experience. In order to work with the mind, though, we need to understand how it functions.

GETTING TO KNOW YOUR MIND

Observe your mind, so you can get a better idea of how it functions.

- Sit comfortably. Don't try to think about anything, but just watch the thoughts arise and fall in the mind without getting involved in thinking about the thoughts, just observe.

- Take a few moments to just observe thoughts as they arise.

- Notice thoughts that begin with "I like" or "I don't like" and then notice the thoughts that follow those statements.

....

The goal is to get used to noticing the arising of the "I like" or "I don't like" thoughts. You can do this as you go about your day in almost any situation. Watch how this entire process of thinking works to carry you away from the present moment.

OUR WILD, WANDERING MIND

When most of us try the above exercise, we're surprised by how little control we seem to have over our own mind. Normally, we become so overwhelmed by the cascade of thoughts that rush by, it's really hard just to notice our thinking process without getting lost in the thoughts. What does getting lost mean? It means rather than staying present in the mere observation of thoughts, we become so engrossed in thinking about them that we forget all about our intention to simply notice.

Isn't it totally wild that even though we intend to simply observe our thought process, we almost immediately are distracted by it? We think a thought, and then think about that thought, and then think about each thought that follows, until after a while we realize we are not there anymore.

The first thing we need to do, in order to be radically happy, is to gain control, or mastery, over this wild, wandering mind and bring our attention into the present moment. Since our mind belongs only to us, shouldn't we be able to control it? When we have control over our mind, we can make a conscious decision whether to allow our mind to wander or not. We have the ability to drop the habit of chasing after our thoughts and emotions, likes and dislikes, and instead choose to become completely engaged in the moment, just as it is. Since we are the ones who taught ourselves the habit of chasing after our thoughts and emotions, we can develop a habit of being in the present moment, undistracted by those thoughts and emotions.

CREATING SPACE

During the day, we have so many things running through our heads: we may think about how to hook up with that super-interesting new person we run into at the café every morning; how to get ahead in our career, working around difficult and annoying colleagues; dinner plans with friends; or how to find some down time. And that's only what came up between getting out of bed and breakfast! The list can seem so long that we can feel like there isn't enough time in the day to deal with even a small portion of what our mind is cooking up.

Some days it seems like our mind gets sucked into each and every problem that comes our way, and then our perspective begins to shrink. Suddenly, we might even find ourselves in a world where problems seem to be many and possibilities for resolution seem to be few. Our minds begin to loop over and over our predicament, without any resolution. The same worries go through our head over and over again, tormenting us, and taking us further and further away from the present moment and any chance for lasting contentment.

As you probably experienced in the first exercise, it is really hard to just be present and watch the mind. The wandering-mind habit is so well entrenched that we almost immediately become engrossed in thinking rather than watching the thinking. Before we can learn how to be fully present we need to be able to give ourselves a break from this constant habit of thinking about thoughts. If you are able to weaken this habit, even a little, you will begin to know what your mind is like when it isn't helplessly imprisoned by an endless cycle of chasing one thought with another and another.

· · · · · · · PHAKCHOK RINPOCHE · · · · · · ·

Several years ago, while I was in England on an annual teaching tour, someone called me from my home in Nepal saying that some of my students weren't getting along. They were creating big problems for themselves and everyone around them. This news really irritated me, and the more I thought about it the more I became completely fed up with the entire situation. I just kept thinking over and over, "Why is it always like this? Why are they doing this?! How am I going to deal with these problems when I'm on the other side of the world? What's going to happen now?" And on and on and on went my thought process. Ironically, these thoughts were spinning around and around in my head while I was sitting in the car on my way to give a public talk called "The Key to Happiness." When I considered that fact, I became even more irritated with myself and I thought, "What a joke this is! If I can't be happy myself, how on earth can I teach others about happiness?"

Then I stopped thinking for a while and just stared out of the car window at the passing scenery. Thankfully we were driving through the open countryside, on a clear day, with a wide-open blue sky overhead. I had about twenty minutes before we reached the venue, so I gazed out and let my mind blend with the spacious sky. Inspired by the vastness and beauty of the sky, I closed my eyes and imagined I was surrounded by space. After just a few minutes, I experienced a sense of relief. The irritation and tightness subsided, a sense of spaciousness and ease emerged, and the problems that had been troubling me so much seemed small and no longer overwhelming. In fact, I quickly found myself jotting down a few ideas on how the misunderstanding between my students could be resolved.

. . . .

When our mind is tight, any thought that arises dominates. When our mind feels spacious, then no thought that arises can completely take us over. It's like the difference between a tiny 10-by-10-foot room and a huge 100-by-100-foot room. In the tiny room, anything you place there completely defines it. If you put a desk in there, it's an office. If you put a bed in there, it's a bedroom. If you put a stove in, it's a kitchen. In a huge room, you can have many things, and different environments, yet no single thing defines the room. When we create space, thoughts and emotions can still appear, but they no longer completely define our state of mind.

The Creating Space exercise is an excellent way to deal with our stress and looping thoughts. It can relieve the tension and uptightness in our mind and also in our body. Creating space is a very simple method that interrupts our habitual patterns of thinking about thoughts and emotions. It is the basis for many of the subsequent exercises in this book. It is really important to learn how to create space, in our mind and in our lives.

Why not try it out now? It isn't necessary to spend lots of time on the following exercise. Even five minutes is enough, but ten is even better!

CREATING SPACE

- Sit comfortably and close your eyes.

- Imagine being surrounded by an infinite, perfectly clear, blue sky. The sky is cloudless, spacious, pristine, the deepest sky-blue color. It completely envelops you, extending ceaselessly in every direction— above, below, and to every side. There are no walls, no boundaries, and no buildings, nothing at all in any direction.

- Continue resting your mind on this infinite sky by making the experience of spaciousness as vivid and vibrant in your mind's eye as possible.

- If you become lost in thinking about work, things you need to do, or anything really, that's normal. Just gently return your attention to imagining boundless space.

- Having created a sky as vividly and clearly as possible, spend some time appreciating the space you've imagined. Do this by feeling the spacious quality of the sky. Appreciate the beauty of the space you're imagining and how infinitely vast, spacious, and immaculate the sky around you is. You don't have to go on and on about it. Just gently try to feel how it is to be in the spaciousness of the sky.

- Allow yourself to feel the spaciousness permeating everywhere: inside and outside your body and the mind.

- Rest for a little while in this feeling.

- Slowly open your eyes and reorient yourself to your surroundings.

How do you feel? Consider trying this out for at least five minutes a day for the next week before moving on to the next exercise.

When you are beginning to learn to be fully present and undistracted, it can be very hard not to become carried away by your thoughts and emotions. It can be especially hard if you have a lot of stress or pressure in your life—and these days, who doesn't? By creating space, you're shifting your attention away from the normal patterns of thinking and emotional reactions. Through the strength of your imagination, you generate a powerfully effective mental and emotional environment: even if turbulent thoughts and emotions arise, they won't be able to distract you.

Most of us lead incredibly hectic lives, between long hours at work and all of our personal responsibilities, so it is hard to feel very spacious. This is why we recommend creating space, so you can get used to feeling spaciousness, both during the meditation session and in normal daily life. But, in order not to become too spaced out, remain mindful of your mental image of space, and use your awareness to maintain the mindfulness. Don't become lost in space. Simply be mindful of your sense of spaciousness.

CREATING SPACE IS NOT THE SAME AS CREATING DISTANCE

After being introduced to the Creating Space exercise, people often have an impression that the point of the practice is to get some distance from our problems. This is not the case. "Creating distance" is usually a process of avoiding or pushing away the things that make us feel uncomfortable. Creating space, on the other hand, is a way to slow down or interrupt our habitual way of reacting to these situations.

When we're stressed out, it's usually a sign that we don't have enough space in our lives. At these times we often experience this as a feeling of being constricted or boxed in. We can become so anxious that it begins to manifest physically. It might emerge, for example, as tightness in our chest or shallow breathing. At such times, we often let out a big sigh to try to release the tension. This tight, boxed-in feeling serves little positive function in our lives. It can lead to a shortsighted, reactionary, or closed-minded state, because we are controlled by our habits and negative emotions. When we create space, the very spaciousness itself becomes the focus of our mind, and the tension in our mind and body will begin to naturally relax. Spaciousness gives our mind the room to see more possibilities, to be calm and considered in our actions, and ultimately to make more informed decisions than we otherwise would be able to.

Through the practice of creating space we can begin to experience true freedom from our habitual way of reacting. We can safely look at our problems without succumbing to habitual patterns of hope and fear. We don't have to reject them, push them away, or struggle with them. We don't need to obsessively dwell on each problem, reacting to its every aspect with tension and emotion. Rather, while sustaining a spacious mind, we can observe it and even learn to work through it, utilizing the strength and intelligence of a spacious and calm mind.

It's interesting how many important insights have come when some of history's greatest thinkers took a moment to relax. Archimedes figured out how to tell if the king was cheated only after he stopped thinking and got in the bath. Newton had his big insight about gravitation when he "sat in a contemplative mood" and an apple fell from a tree. Niels Bohr's Nobel Prize–winning insight came to him as he was drifting off to sleep. Paul McCartney came up with "Yesterday," one of the most recorded songs in history, just as he was waking up. The list goes on and on. No doubt these insights were the fruition of a long process of concentration and thought, but the results emerged only after the mind was given a chance to relax.

Take a moment to reflect on your life. Did you make your best decisions when you were feeling really anxious or fearful or when you were feeling calm and spacious? Did your best, most creative and fruitful ideas come when you were relaxed and at ease or when you were consumed with irritation and worry?

So it is really a good idea to create some space in your mind; by calming your mind, even a little bit, you will discover there is more space not only in your mind but in your life. You will have more space to think about the things that really need thinking about. So create some space every day. Get to know your mind free from the turmoil of looping thoughts and emotions.

PART ONE

BASIC HAPPINESS

Mastering the Mind

The key to basic happiness is to get used to being fully present in the moment, just as it is. The more we are able to be in the present moment, the less the ingrained habit of *thinking about thoughts* will have the power to distract us.

THE THREE KEYS TO BASIC HAPPINESS

1. Always react to thoughts the same way.

The practice of meditation is an incredibly effective way to become more and more familiar with remaining present. While meditating, we practice reacting to whatever comes to our mind in the exact same way—no matter what sensations, thoughts, or emotions arise, we do not follow after them. Instead of thinking about them, we remain anchored, fully present in the moment.

2. Relax the comparing.

The involuntary habit of constantly evaluating experience distracts us and makes it difficult to fully enjoy even life's simplest pleasures. But it gets worse. These thoughts build upon and reinforce each other. They grow into the world's biggest stealer of contentment—comparing ourselves to others and their circumstances. We can relax the comparing by learning to accept ourselves, warts and all. We can learn to appreciate what we have.

3. Be present.

Through the practice of meditation we turn our attention toward the present moment. But we have to be able to bring the awareness of the present moment from the meditation cushion into ordinary everyday experience. That way, when things are going well, we can drop most of our usual strategies for trying to keep the good times rolling and instead just be present and enjoy. Also when disaster strikes, we won't completely lose our equanimity and become depressed. The whole point of meditation practice is to become so familiar with the state of non-distraction that we can integrate the be-present experience into whatever we are doing.

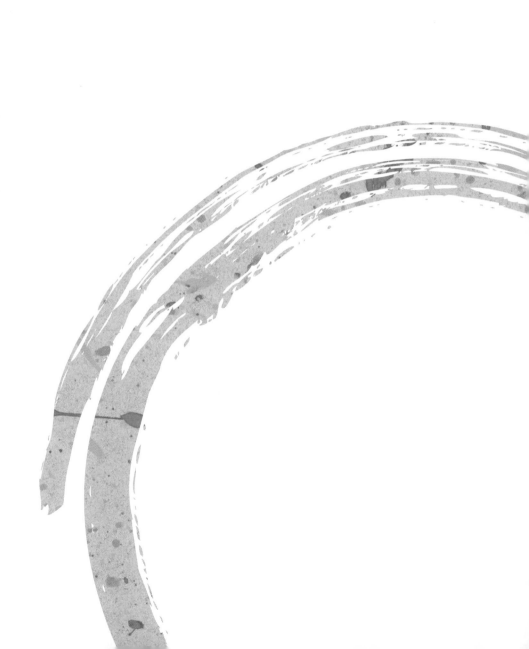

CHAPTER 4

Always React to Thoughts the Same Way

As we go about our everyday life, we are perpetually reacting to our thoughts. If we like something, we want to keep it or prolong it. If we think of something we don't like, we worry about how to avoid it or get rid of it. Nearly every thought that comes into our head gets special attention, with a reaction tailor-made for it. By contrast, in meditation practice, we learn to always react to every thought the same way—instead of thinking about it and setting off a chain of thoughts that could go in many different directions, we keep our attention on the present moment. At first we need to meditate to get used to being fully present. But over time, we will need to be able to carry the present-focused mind into any situation.

Through meditation practice we can train our mind in such a way that our attention remains *wherever we place it*. And in order to experience basic happiness we want to be able to place our mind in the present moment, rather than habitually thinking about one thought after another.

FOCUSING ON THE BREATH

Practicing creating space is a first step toward experiencing basic happiness. While we are creating space, we can experience a break from any tension and looping thoughts that were crowding in on us. They may still be lurking in our mind, but they no longer define how we feel. Creating space gives us a taste of the natural mental peace and steadiness that is uncovered once our thoughts and emotions lose their power to carry us away from the present moment. Wouldn't it be wonderful to experience this peace in any situation?

The Creating Space exercise needs to be practiced in special sessions, as it can be quite challenging to keep imagining space while being active in the world. The following meditation practices are designed to progressively help us gain familiarity with just being present, so that we can do it in any situation.

Learning to meditate while focusing on our breath will help to bring us into the present moment. And, unlike creating space, with a little practice we can learn to place our attention on our breath in many different situations.

FOCUSING ON THE BREATH

- Sit comfortably on a chair or cushion, with your back straight.

- To calm the mind, begin by doing the Creating Space exercise. Relax and experience a feeling of spaciousness, then open your eyes.

- Leave your eyes open, with a relaxed and natural gaze into the space in front of you. There is no need to focus or rest the gaze upon anything.

- Now, gently bring your attention to the rhythm of your breath.

- As you breathe out, just know that you are breathing out; as you breathe in, just know that you are breathing in. Focus lightly on the breath, without intensely fixating or making a lot of effort. Employ the same light-handed effort you would use to pick up a glass of water or a pen.

- Remain aware of everything, but keep your attention lightly on your breath. The moment you find that your attention has drifted away, gently return to your breath. Whatever thoughts or emotions arise in the mind, always react the same way by placing your attention on the breath.

- Body still, speech silent, and mind lightly following the rhythm of inhalation and exhalation, just as it naturally occurs, there is no need to block any thoughts or emotions that may arise. Just keep noticing the breath. Thoughts come, stay with the breath; thoughts go, rest your mind gently upon the breath. Present and aware, steadily keep your attention on the breath.

- After a while, you may realize you've become lost in thinking about thoughts and have completely forgotten about the breath. At that very moment, gently bring your attention to rest once again on the breath.

That's how simple and easy meditation can be. Try spending ten minutes each day practicing focusing on the breath. It's a good idea to start by doing several minutes of creating space beforehand. This could be especially helpful if you have a lot on your mind or have a lot of stress in your life. When practicing focusing on the breath, there is no need to analyze how you became distracted or to scold yourself. Instead, in the very moment you realize you have become distracted, simply bring your attention back to the breath. There is no good or bad, no need for mental commentary on how your meditation is going. All that needs to be done is to notice whether or not your attention is resting on the breath.

WHY MEDITATION WORKS—GIVING OUR MIND A JOB

In Tibetan, the word for meditation is *gom*. Gom literally means "getting familiar with" or "getting used to." By practicing meditation in the way explained in this book, you can get used to remaining present, undisturbed by whatever thoughts or emotions arise in your mind.

As you can now tell, meditation is a process of getting to know how our mind works and training our attention to rest where we place it, but you might still wonder: Why do we need to train our mind? Can't we just decide to pay attention and that's it?

That would be great, but our mind normally behaves like an excited monkey, jumping from place to place. It just does. Our mind thinks about this and then it thinks about that. We sit down to meditate and at first we are present, watching our breath. But, after a few moments we are lost in a daydream, thinking about thoughts. We may have started out by watching the breath, but soon we are on an island enjoying a piña colada at the beach and next we are thinking about all the money we have to save to get there. Before long, several minutes have passed and we realize we forgot all about the breath. The monkey mind jumps here and there almost without stopping.

Nearly everything we do is a result of what our mind is thinking. Our monkey mind is constantly talking to us and telling us what to do, and we don't know how to guide it. Our mind is under our control to some degree, but a few minutes on the meditation cushion should convince us of how little control we actually have over it.

When the monkey mind tells us something, we react in one of two ways: we follow it, or we fight with it and try to push it away.

If our mind tells us something is good and we want it, we follow our mind. Or perhaps our mind is telling us how funny our partner looks in that outfit, but we struggle with ourselves not to mention it and try to push the thought away.

Some people think meditation is about siting there, clearing the mind by blocking thoughts and emotions. They struggle with their mind, thinking, "I must meditate, I must keep a quiet mind, no emotions, and CONCENTRATE!" Other people try to meditate by blissing out, thinking meditation is all about peace, openness, and reaching a special level of consciousness. They try to cultivate a particular state of mind.

Meditation is about neither cultivating nor rejecting but rather about learning how to be present in the face of whatever rises in our mind. Yet, in the beginning, we may need to calm our mind in order to not become overwhelmed and distracted by our thoughts. That is why we recommend creating space to calm the mind. Eventually, as we gain experience, we will actually be able to use turbulent thoughts as a support for our meditation, which is pretty radical, isn't it? Until then, we need to be able to settle our mind. But once our mind settles, we don't have to remain in a tightly focused state of concentration, nor do we have to create a blissful experience.

If we are too tight, we are blocking our senses, and that can be quite an exhausting struggle. When we are too open and relaxed, we may feel good, but this can easily result in strengthening our fondness for creating experiences, the basis of all our trouble. Whether we prefer a state of control or creating a pleasant state of openness, we are still worried about circumstances, even if they are just mental states. The mind is naturally open; we don't need to do anything to open it up. If the mind weren't already open, nothing would be able to appear in the mind. Yet everything that appears to us, appears in the mind. Otherwise, how else would we know about it? We don't need to block out or cultivate anything. We just need to get used to remaining present: aware of—yet undistracted by—whatever sights, sounds, sensations, thoughts, and emotions appear.

Think about having a party. If you're an experienced host, when you have a difficult, disruptive guest, you won't immediately argue with the guest and try to throw him out. That could easily ruin the evening for everyone. Instead, you will flatter and schmooze your guest, find common ground, and give him something pleasant to do. Perhaps you offer him his favorite drink (unless he's already had one too many), a plate of the tastiest food you have, or the most comfortable chair to relax in. Once given the space to relax, the guest becomes more agreeable, more open to suggestion.

We don't have to fight with the monkey-like, restless quality of our mind, nor do we have to follow it around getting completely lost in thoughts. The monkey mind needs something to do, or it starts creating all kinds of problems. So, let's give the monkey mind something to do. Let's be a good host.

So, first we tell the monkey mind to pay attention to the breath moving in and out, and for a few moments it behaves, but then monkey mind thinks something like "Piña coladas are so delicious!" and we become distracted. But we don't need to get mad and rigid, morphing into a strict disciplinarian. We just gently remind the monkey mind that its job is to focus on the breath.

In this way, we gradually tame the restless monkey mind. Our mind becomes more pliable and more workable. Negative thoughts and emotions hold less and less sway over us. This is the actual fruit of meditation: mastering our mind. Calmness of mind may be a nice side effect, but the real fruit of meditation practice is that our mind becomes more and more flexible and less and less a prisoner to habitual ways of reacting. We are able to place our attention where we want, and thoughts and emotions, while still arising, won't distract us. We can choose to follow them if it suits our needs, but we are no longer blown about, like a leaf in the wind, as each thought or emotion breezes through.

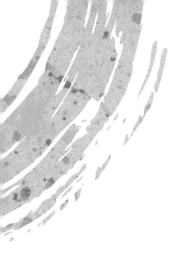

> # Don't just do something,
> # sit there!
>
> —Sylvia Boorstein

MEDITATION WITH AN OBJECT

As you begin meditation practice, as we've demonstrated above, the discipline of the practice is to bring your attention to an object and leave it there. If you become distracted, simply bring your mind back to the object. Using the example of the monkey mind, give the monkey mind the job of remaining mindful of the object of your meditation. By remaining mindful of the object, the monkey mind stops jumping all over the place. This means that you will interrupt the habit of following after every thought and emotion that rises in your mind. Instead, no matter what thought or emotion comes to mind always react the same way by returning your attention to the object of your meditation.

You might wonder, what do we mean by an "object"? So far, we have used two kinds of objects for our meditation: our breath and space. In the latter example, we use our mind to create an infinite sky, and we keep our attention on space. But we can use anything as an object: sights, sounds, sensations, even thoughts.

By bringing our attention back to the object, again and again and yet again, gradually the monkey mind calms down; we become more and more settled in the present moment, undistracted by any thoughts or emotions that pass through our mind. This is the goal of using an object for our meditation practice: to be fully present in the moment. It is what we mean when we say non-distraction.

MEDITATION WITHOUT AN OBJECT

As you become more and more familiar with non-distraction, you will find that you can drop the method of using an object. Eventually, non-distraction itself is all the support you need for meditation practice. This is called *meditation without an object*.

To understand why we can meditate without an object to meditate on, it's important to appreciate what non-distraction really means. First, it is important to point out that it is not a state that we cultivate or create, it is a natural quality of our mind. Usually we don't notice it since it is normally obscured by our thoughts and emotions. In other words, when we no longer allow our attention to be carried away by a chain of thoughts, non-distraction is revealed. It is where we rest in the natural awareness of our own mind, free from the distraction of rising thoughts and emotions.

This awareness is pure knowing, without having to be aware of something. Our minds are naturally aware, but usually we are distracted by what we are aware of. And we start to think about it in an endless cycle of thoughts. But awareness itself does not need those things in order to be aware. If you are following thoughts and emotions, involuntarily thinking about them, that is what is meant by being distracted. When we rest in awareness itself, that is non-distraction. It isn't a blank state. We can be aware of everything around us, but non-distraction doesn't depend on an object in order to be aware.

We get our first direct experience of this awareness whenever we're practicing meditation with an object and we realize we've become distracted. That moment of knowing we've become distracted is the arising of awareness that is naturally free of thoughts and emotions. Of course, we may also have the thought "I am distracted." But that is a thought, not the knowing awareness itself. In other words, we know we are distracted whether we have the thought or not. If we have the thought "I am distracted," awareness notices the thought. And then, as we return our attention to the breath or whatever object we are using as a meditation support, we return to meditation. However, if we instead follow the thought, we return to distraction.

Normally, we mentally grasp on to objects by thinking about them. We constantly evaluate experiences and try to grasp after the things we like. We also can try avoiding them, but, ironically, that is grasping too! So, in meditation, we use this habitual tendency to grasp in a way that skillfully relaxes the grasping habit. We do that simply by using an object to be mindful of. Mindfulness practice uses the monkey mind's habit of grasping in a special way that allows the grasping itself to naturally relax.

We use our natural awareness to make sure we are being mindful. This has two purposes:

1.
It keeps the grasping monkey mind busy
(by being mindful) so that it can't distract us, and

2.
It allows us to gradually become
more and more familiar with awareness itself.
The more familiar we become with our awareness,
the more we enter into non-distraction.

RELAXED SPACIOUSNESS

There are two main aspects of meditation that we've just been discussing: mindfulness and awareness.

There is also a third aspect we need to bring into our meditation practice—relaxed spaciousness. We may have already become little bit familiar with it through the Creating Space exercise. It is an essential part of any meditation practice. If our mind is too tight in meditation, we become overly concerned with holding the object of meditation in mind. Then meditation becomes just an ordinary practice of grasping the object and avoiding forgetting about the object. But when we bring in a relaxed, spacious attitude, we don't have to block anything or grasp too tightly. We allow our natural awareness to maintain mindfulness, but we don't chase thoughts and emotions away. Just like when the skillful host gives the difficult guest a little space so she can relax, we allow thoughts and emotions the space to rise and then fall naturally away. We spaciously bring our attention back to the object, and the rest takes care of itself: the power of thoughts to distract us naturally dissipates.

There is a famous story about a monk named Shrona who asked the Buddha the best way to meditate. The Buddha asked Shrona, who had been a musician before he was a monk, what was the best way to get the sound out of his instrument: "Was it when the strings were very tight or when they were very loose?" Shrona answered, "Neither, the best sound came when the strings were neither too loose nor too tight." Buddha rejoined, "It's the same for your mind in meditation; it should be neither too concentrated nor too relaxed."

In the same way, while our attitude should be spacious and relaxed in meditation, we needn't be so relaxed that we just daydream, listlessly following one thought after the other. We need to remain aware and keep returning our attention to the object. Yet if we are rigidly mindful, blocking everything else from rising in our mind, we will never become familiar with awareness and will still be distracted by our habit of becoming obsessed with objects we like and dislike.

For the rest of this chapter, we will explore different kinds of objects we can use to bring us into the present moment. Any sensation at all either can be a distraction or can be used to bring us back to the present moment. Gradually, as we become more and more familiar with remaining in non-distraction, we can drop the method. At that point, we no longer need an object. The only "object" we need is awareness itself. We rest our mind in its own naturally spacious, mindful awareness, free from ordinary thoughts and emotions. We'll look at meditating without using an object at the end of the book.

USING SIGHTS, SOUNDS, AND PHYSICAL SENSATIONS AS AN OBJECT

SIGHT

LEARNING TO MEDITATE WITH YOUR EYES OPEN

Some people wonder why we recommend meditating with eyes open. When people are first learning meditation, they often say it's easier to remain undistracted if their eyes are closed. It's okay if one needs to begin sessions with eyes closed, but it is actually quite important to learn to meditate with eyes open.

Through meditation practice we learn to stay fully present, undistracted by thoughts and emotions. The more and more familiar we become with non-distraction, the more and more likely it becomes that non-distraction becomes our normal way of being. So, we needn't leave meditative awareness behind just because we get up from our seat. We can become familiar enough with non-distraction so that we remain in that way while we are performing our job, doing household chores, making love, partying with our friends, or even writing strange books.

Getting used to being completely present and aware in the face of whatever thoughts, emotions, sights, smells, or sounds arise, is what meditation is really all about. By closing our eyes, we are subtly perpetuating the habit of avoiding and cultivating particular circumstances. We end up trying to avoid visual sensations in order

to be completely in the present moment. In fact, visual forms can *support* our meditation practice. We can use them to bring us into the present moment.

If we can be completely undistracted only when we close our eyes, how will we be able to do it as we move through our day? So we need to either get accustomed to meditating with open eyes or learn to do all our daily activities with our eyes shut. Which seems more difficult?

In this meditation practice, we give ourselves something to look at by resting our gaze on an object. We can use any object, but it usually works out better if it is a pleasant object, for example, a candle, a flower, or a beautiful nature photo. We can also use a sacred object such as a religious icon if that helps to inspire us to sit.

Usually it is best if the object isn't too complex or busy. The idea is that we will keep our attention and our gaze lightly resting on the object, without indulging in thinking about the object.

LOOKING AT AN OBJECT

- Sit in a comfortable meditation posture.

- Begin by doing the Creating Space exercise. When you feel that your mind has started to settle, gently open your eyes.

- Rest your gaze on the object. Allow the object to be the focus of your attention.

- It isn't necessary to focus intently on every detail, but just rest your gaze upon form, without having to think about it.

- If you notice your mind beginning to wander, lost in thoughts, gently bring your attention back to the object.

- Lightly rest your attention on the object for the duration of your meditation session.

That's it! If you are having a lot of trouble meditating with your eyes open here's one way to get used to it: Rest your gaze lightly on an object like a flower or a candle. Gently keep your attention on the object. If that begins to be too distracting, close your eyes. Spend some time focusing on the breath. Then, when you're ready, open your eyes, and start afresh.

You can try this practice instead of focusing on the breath or you can focus on the breath for five minutes and then use an image. Or vice versa. It's best if you can spend a few minutes creating space first.

SOUND

USING SOURCES OF DISTRACTION AS
A SUPPORT FOR MEDITATION

• • • • • • • PHAKCHOK RINPOCHE • • • • • • •

When I was a teenager, I often reacted quite strongly and negatively to loud sounds coming from the streets outside our home. The endless sound of Kathmandu construction, banging, big trucks, and human voices would drive me crazy. I could forget about even trying to meditate while all this racket was going on.

But then my teacher suggested I start using sound as a support for my meditation practice. This changed everything. After some years I can say that sounds rarely bother me anymore. In fact, sounds that I used to think of as annoying instead strengthen my mindfulness. And now loud sounds, in any situation, don't bother me.

Now when I hear the same loud sound, without thinking about it, I meditate quietly. I found the overwhelming sound naturally brought me into meditation practice. The sound itself simply reminded me to be completely present.

• • • • • • • • • • •

People often say that they can't meditate because there is too much noise, or their body is uncomfortable. We naturally think of sights, sounds, tactile sensations, tastes, and smells as sources of distraction that take us away from meditation. However, we can learn how to work with those things that we normally think of as sources of distraction, and transform them into supports for our practice.

We can use any of the five senses as a way of supporting our practice. For example, rather than evaluating whether or not we find a sound distracting or pleasant, we can just use the sensation of sound as the object of our meditation.

EXERCISE 5

USING THE
SENSATION
OF SOUND

- Start by spending a few minutes creating space.

- Now bring your attention to the sensation of sound. Put your awareness in your ears.

- Simply be aware of any sounds that you hear.

- Notice how a sound arises and then fades away.

- There is no need to think about what kind of sound it is, or whether it is pleasant or obnoxious.

- If you notice that you have become lost in thinking, at that moment, gently return your attention to the sensation of sound.

....

Note: If the sound is really painfully loud, that is probably an indication that you need to protect your hearing. Then it is appropriate to consider either putting in earplugs or meditating elsewhere.

SMELL & TASTE

USING THE SENSE OF SMELL AND TASTE

By now you are probably getting the gist of how any sensation—sight, sound, or tactile—can be used as a support for meditation. Odors can be used as a support just like any other sensation. If there is a strong smell in the room, rather than allowing it to become a source for more distracted thinking, we can rest our attention lightly upon it.

Taste, on the other hand, is usually a dominant sense only when we eat or drink something. When we are eating or drinking something, allow the sensation to bring you fully into the present moment. Lightly focus your attention on the taste. This is easier to do if you are alone or if the group you are with is willing to engage in mindful gustation.

BODY

WHOLE BODY MEDITATION—USING PHYSICAL SENSATIONS AS A MEDITATION SUPPORT

So far, we've considered using our sight and our hearing as supports. Now, let's extend that to sensations throughout our body as a focus for our attention in meditation practice. This will prepare us for those times where we encounter unpleasant sensations (e.g., backache, knee pain, and so forth) while practicing meditation. And for those of us whose jobs require lots of mental activity, this practice can help us get out of our head and reconnect to our body.

When I used to spend lots of twelve-hour-plus days writing code, at night (or sometimes in the wee hours of the morning) I would be unable to stop thinking about the algorithms I was coding.

Even though most of my best insights would come when I would find a way to take a break from the problem I was working on, sometimes I was unable to disengage, and the same thoughts would loop continuously through my mind.

Sometimes even creating space was too cerebral for me, I was so stuck in my head. But by learning to focus my attention on the sensations in my body, I was gradually able to become more present-moment focused.

· · · · · · · · · · ·

Mindful awareness isn't just about remaining present in the face of whatever thoughts and emotions pass through our mind; it is also about remaining present in the face of any sensation. For example, after sitting for a while, we might have a slight pain in our back. Normally, we regard this pain as an annoyance that interrupts our practice, distracting us from meditating. Instead we can use this uncomfortable sensation as the object that we rest our attention on.

We need to be aware of what we are feeling both mentally *and* physically. The body scan gets us out of our head by placing our attention on our body. We start at the top of our head and gradually move our attention down, feeling every part of our body.

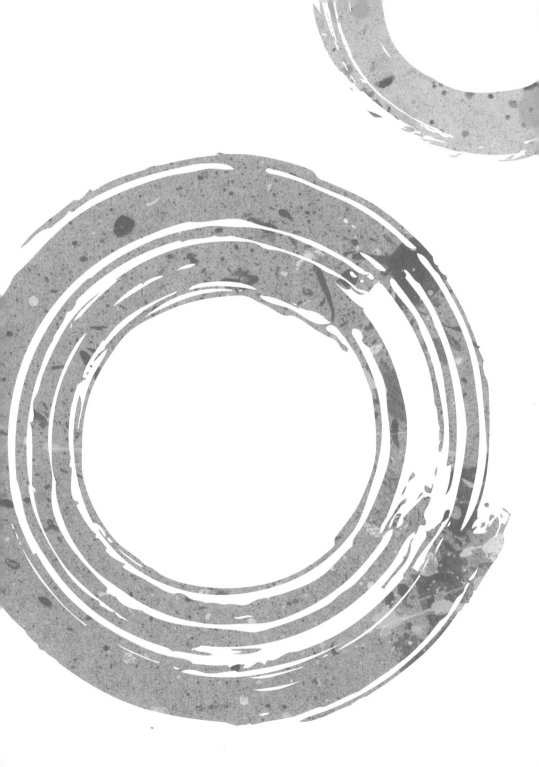

BODY SCAN

- Begin the practice by sitting in an upright comfortable position.

- Spend a few minutes creating space.

- After a minute or two, gently bring your attention to the crown of your head. Notice any sensation you may feel. Just observe, try not to engage in thinking about whether the sensations are pleasant or not.

- Now gradually bring your attention down to your forehead, notice any sensations that you might have. Allow yourself to simply be aware of any sensation on your forehead. Just notice, then let go and move on.

- In the same way notice the back of your head, then your face.

- Now bring your attention to your neck.

- Then lower still to your shoulders, upper back. Then down the arms and hands.

- Whatever you notice while scanning down your body, just rest there for a moment and move on. Don't grasp on to anything or work to stay mindful. Just by noticing, letting go, and moving on you will gradually become more and more present-moment focused.

- Slowly, gradually scan down your body. Notice the feeling of the seat you are sitting on, any muscle tightness you may have, and how your clothes feel against your skin.

- Finally when you reach the tips of your toes, drop the practice and just relax. If you like you can remain focusing on the breath for a few minutes.

....

While you can also do this practice from the bottom up, if you have a lot of looping or fast-moving thoughts, it is usually better to start at the top and scan downward. Practicing this way usually calms the mind.

PAIN
(USING) DISCOMFORT AND PAIN

Normally, when we experience pain, discomfort, or even an itch during meditation we react in either of two ways:

One way is to try to avoid it by shifting our position, touching the area of the body experiencing the sensation. The other is that we try to ignore it, which unfortunately usually results in a single-pointed preoccupation with the sensation. Then we become completely distracted, lost in thoughts about the discomfort.

This just makes the pain or itch almost impossible to bear.

Instead of making the discomfort the object of your thoughts, you can make it the object of your meditation. Instead of trying to ignore the pain, the itch, the feeling of being chilly or too hot, you can engage the mind that notices the sensation. You can use the experience itself as a focus of your practice. This counteracts our normal tendency to always try to find peace and happiness in circumstances. Instead of trying to wrestle with the pain or replace it with pleasure, you can change your normal pattern of making the discomfort worse by thinking about it just by simply watching the sensation of discomfort the same way you watch the breath in meditation.

What is amazing about practicing this way is that we no longer need to regard hunger pangs, a twinge in the back, or an itchy chin as a distraction from our meditation. Instead, if you know how to use the sensation, your meditation can become even more stable in present-moment awareness.

Just a note: if you are experiencing severe pain, while you can still use the sensation for practice, it is perhaps a sign of a problem that may also need medical attention.

USING UNCOMFORTABLE SENSATIONS

- When an uncomfortable sensation emerges in your body during meditation, first observe the sensation just as in the Body Scan exercise.

- Simply rest your attention on the sensation itself and not on any thoughts or judgments that may arise about the sensation.

- By resting your awareness lightly on the physical sensation, you can arrive fully present, in meditation, completely undistracted.

- If you notice that you've become distracted, lost in thoughts about the pain or anything else, just bring your attention to rest again on the sensation.

WHICH METHOD TO USE?

At this point, deciding what method of meditation to use might start to seem confusing. The main point is not to flit about from method to method but to choose a method that suits the situation.

It is best if you can start every session by creating space, as this will help to calm the mind. Then you should either focus on the breath or use an image. Use an image if you need help getting used to meditating with your eyes open, or if the image itself inspires meditation. Focusing on the breath is good because discursive thoughts usually rise and fall with our breath, and this method keeps us from getting easily distracted by them. Either method is suitable as a personal basic meditation practice.

When you are following our basic meditation instruction, you may find that you keep getting distracted by a dominant sensory input, such as the sound outside your room or an itchy bugbite. Then you can switch your attention to that sensation. Leave it there for a while. It's not like you hear a sound and use that but ten seconds later switch to the feeling of your backside on the cushion, then jump to smells resulting from your partner cooking in the kitchen. If you flit around like that, you risk supporting discursive thinking rather than being fully present.

No matter what object you choose, you are always using the same essential method: You rest your attention lightly upon an object and leave it there in the face of whatever rises in your mind, be it thoughts, emotions, or physical sensations. No matter what thought or emotion comes into your mind, you always react the same way: gently returning your attention to rest on your meditation object.

CHAPTER 5

Relax
the
Comparing

> Piglet noticed that even though
> he had a Very Small Heart, it could hold
> a rather large amount of Gratitude.
>
> —A. A. Milne

magine you are a teenager on the run from the government. You are persecuted because of your religious beliefs and what you represent, rather than because of any crime you committed. After enormous hardship, living in constant fear, not getting enough to eat, freezing, and so on, you finally find a way to escape.

It's hard to imagine that kind of suffering, isn't it?

· · · · · · · · ERRIC SOLOMON · · · · · · · · ·

My mother's parents didn't speak much about the life they had before coming to the United States. Grandpa first left the pogroms of Belarus for St. Petersburg as a young child, but that eventually didn't work out either. Only when he became quite old, and in response to a lot of prodding from one of my cousins, did he talk much about those years and the traumas he and his family suffered.

I asked Grandpa why he never spoke much about it before. He told me that at the end of the day everyone has difficulties in life, and he didn't think his were so interesting. He explained further that his difficulties led him to life in America, where he was safe and surrounded by family and friends.

When he thought about some of the horrific things he lived through from childhood to his teens, he said that while there is pain in those memories, there is also a lot of gratitude. Because without those earlier experiences he wouldn't have made it to Boston, met Grandma, and had such a satisfying life. In fact, living through those experiences gave him the courage and fortitude to overcome all the other challenges and setbacks that life sometimes threw his way.

· · · · · · · · · · ·

Fortunately, most of us will never have to deal with such extreme and difficult circumstances. Yet, this story points toward an important key to happiness—that rather than dwelling on all that we lack, we can instead focus on whatever it is in our life that is fortunate, even if it pales in comparison to the challenges we face. Don't you find that, far too often, we are comparing our circumstances against other people's more fortunate ones or an idealized version of what we think our life should be like? Does this habit ever bring us joy? When we focus on what we lack, isn't the natural result dissatisfaction and that whatever we have will never seem like enough?

The involuntary habit of constantly evaluating experience distracts us from simply being present, and makes it difficult for us to fully enjoy even life's most basic pleasures. But it gets worse. These thoughts can build upon and reinforce each other. They quickly grow into the world's biggest stealer of contentment: comparing ourselves to others and their circumstances. Even if it isn't others' circumstances, we engage in comparing our life to the life we think we ought to be having. The result of all this comparing can often be thoughts of self-denigration so strong that they overwhelm us even when we try creating space or focusing on the breath. Therefore, we need to *relax the comparing* by learning to accept ourselves, warts and all. We can do that by appreciating what we have. Through gratitude and acceptance, instead of denigrating ourselves, we can approach our shortcomings and improve our lives from the perspective of a healthy self-image.

When I started counting my blessings,
my whole life turned around.

—Willie Nelson, *The Tao of Willie*

We can learn to weaken the habit of comparison by noticing when it arises and replacing it with appreciation. For example, when we are on the beach having a great day, instead of thinking, "too bad we can't have more days like this," we can appreciate how wonderful it is to be able to be here right now. And guess what? This brings us right into the present moment, the place where basic happiness resides.

At this point it is understandable if you are thinking, "You guys are starting to sound like a Hallmark card again! It's important to take stock of my life and to see where I can grow, and dissatisfaction with my circumstances is an opportunity to improve. Dissatisfaction is what spurs me to be successful."

The question isn't whether or not we should ever measure how we are doing in life; we are already doing that most of the time anyway. The question is how much of the time is it habitual, and how often does it result in creating only negative emotions, which can lead to a damaging self-image. Ask yourself, do you always want to be reacting to things from the standpoint of a weak view of yourself or from the point of view afforded by a positive, healthy sense of yourself? Which one will likely lead to the best result? Do you want to be successful and stressed out or could it be that there is a way to be successful and yet *also* relaxed?

· · · · · · · · · ERRIC SOLOMON · · · · · · · · ·

I remember during the first dot-com explosion, it seemed like everyone knew at least one person who was a complete jerk and made $200 million in an IPO (initial public offering of stock, the main way that tech start-ups cash in). For example, there was even one guy at my company whom no one thought was especially talented yet who made megabucks about eighteen months after he quit.

All these stories of overnight gazillionaires totally transformed Silicon Valley; nearly everyone, it seems, was infected by jealousy or extreme dissatisfaction. The funny part was that there were far more people we knew who left their high-paying job for a hundred-hour-a-week start-up that totally flamed out. In other words, a few lucky ones made a lot of money, a few had a good time in spite of or because of the long hours, but most seemed to work like crazy and all they got was a gargantuan dose of stress and even more dissatisfaction.

There were also more than a few people who left a good job because they had a really cool idea and thought it would be fun to try to realize it in the marketplace. It seems to me that those were the ones who were really successful. Some made a boatload of money, but no matter what, they were stoked about the experience. They were grateful that they could get up every day and work on something they believed in.

. . . .

ESTABLISHING A DAILY HABIT OF GRATITUDE

Improving an aspect of your life is easier and more fruitful when you have an attitude of gratitude, rather than when you are obsessed with comparing. We aren't saying *all* comparison is bad (in fact, we're suggesting you engage in a little bit of healthy comparison). The key point is that we need to relax the *habit* of constant comparison.

It's the unconscious habit of comparison we're trying to cut. We need to be able to compare and contrast or we won't be able to function in life. For example, when we go to the grocery store we need to pick out the fresh veggies and avoid the rotting ones. But we also need to be aware of how often we are habitually comparing and understand the way it can steal away our sense of well-being. So, comparison is okay, just as long as it is a conscious act and not the habitual comparison that's the result of constantly evaluating the quality of experience, the thing that robs us of basic happiness.

In the following exercises, you will be given an opportunity to develop an attitude of gratitude. Each one builds on the one before, so it is good to repeat each exercise until you feel comfortable with it before moving on to the next.

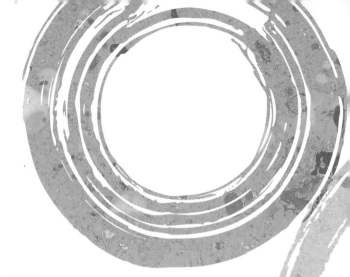

HAPPY WITH HOW I AM AND WHAT I HAVE

It's best if you can do this exercise at the beginning of the day. You can make it part of your normal meditation practice.

- Begin the practice by sitting in an upright comfortable position.

- Start by creating space for a few minutes.

- As you breathe in, think, "I am happy with who I am." As you exhale, think, "I am happy with what I have."

- Repeat this breathing exercise at least twenty-one times. Then, start your normal meditation practice.

APPRECIATING A QUALITY OR POSSESSION

We can begin each day by recalling a reason to appreciate something about our life, such as a quality of ourselves that we like or something we have that we appreciate. Don't think that anything is too insignificant to appreciate. Even simple things like "I really enjoy the first coffee of the day" or "I love my new hoodie" are a good way to do this exercise. It is also good to think of something about ourselves that we are satisfied with. For example, we could pick something we did such as an act of kindness, a moment of insight, or a quality we have. It could be the way we were able to figure out a solution to a vexing problem or something simple like the way we were able to make a stranger smile. Here's how it works.

- Just before you go to bed, think of one possession or quality in your life that you appreciate. Write it down, and place it where you like to practice in the morning.

- When you wake up do five to ten minutes of creating space (more is okay too!).

- Do the Happy with How I Am and What I Have exercise twenty-one times.

- Read your note of appreciation and cultivate a feeling of gratitude by reflecting on it.

- Practice meditation with an object (e.g., the Focusing on the Breath or Looking at an Object exercises) for a few minutes.

APPRECIATING CIRCUMSTANCES

This is exactly like the previous exercise except you are picking a circumstance in your life you really appreciate. For example, you can appreciate basic things such as where you live or the fact that you have enough to eat. Maybe you have a favorite pub or café you like to hang out at, a vacation that you are looking forward to, or maybe your favorite sports team won an important game. It really can be anything positive. There are all sorts of circumstances you can have gratitude for.

As you have heard us say before, we aren't against enjoying the good things that happen, so have a little gratitude and enjoy. But there is also a catch here. We have to be careful not to make the object of our appreciation a comparison with others' circumstances. An example of this would be "I am glad I am not starving like the unfortunate people in that other drought-stricken country." We can just appreciate that we have enough to eat without reflecting on someone else's misfortune. We are trying to transform our habit of habitually comparing ourselves to others or an idealized version of ourselves. So even though these kinds of thoughts about "how I am not suffering like my grandmother did when she was a refugee" are a potential source of gratitude, they actually reinforce the very habit we are trying to dissolve—the habit of comparing our circumstances to someone else's.

CELEBRATING THE MEDITATION SESSION

The very endeavor to create space, meditate, or do gratitude practice is itself a reason to celebrate. You can bring to mind the benefits of learning to simply be present, and take a moment to enjoy the very fact that you are taking time to care for your mind and spirit.

- Just before you are ready to end your session, appreciate and celebrate that you made the time to practice and reflect on the good qualities of your efforts.

- Do something to support this celebration, like read a paragraph from a book that inspires you, read something online about the benefits of meditation practice, or read an entry from your gratitude journal (see next page).

NO TIME TO MEDITATE?

You can of course skip the Creating Space exercise or meditation parts of each exercise above. Gratitude practice won't be as effective, but it is still better than not doing it. Just start your day with the thought "I am happy with who I am, I am happy with what I have." If you have time, you can also bring to mind one thing in your life you really appreciate.

A GRATITUDE JOURNAL

It's good if you can write your daily gratitude thought from the Appreciating a Quality or Possession or Appreciating Circumstances exercises in a journal or notepad. At the end of each week, instead of coming up with a new thing to appreciate, read through your collected moments of gratitude from the previous six days and reflect.

MEDITATE, DON'T EVALUATE: AGENDALESS MEDITATION

At some point, most of us start rating the quality of our meditation practice. We think things like "today my meditation practice is so calm and peaceful" or perhaps "What is going wrong? I can't seem to calm my mind. I feel so agitated!" At first glance it seems perfectly reasonable that we check in to see how our meditation is going. But actually, this habit of constantly evaluating our experience is exactly what we are supposed to be free of when we are meditating. It is tempting to constantly compare how our practice is with how we think it is supposed to be, but this kind of comparison won't help. While meditating, no matter what thoughts arise, we should always react the same way: just let the thoughts be and return our attention to the breath or whatever object we are using as a support for our practice. Agendaless meditation is another way we can relax the comparing.

So, how then can we measure our progress? After the meditation session has been completed, it is a good idea to reflect on how our practice was. Maybe we were too relaxed and our mind seemed a little dull. Or perhaps we kept forgetting what we were doing and were constantly agitated, lost in thinking about our day. In such cases, we should make a mental note. Over time we can develop a deeper understanding of our mental habits during meditation, which we can bring to future sessions.

Sometimes you will notice that your meditation went really well. That's great. Take a moment to enjoy the feeling. Notice how your body feels, the details of the place you are meditating (outdoors, indoors, which room, and so on), and any other sounds or smells. Take a moment to reflect on how your mind feels. A vivid recollection of what it feels like when your practice goes well can inspire you later on if you bring the memory to mind at the start of a session. (We explain how to use a memory of a calm meditation experience to overcome anxiety in the "Mini-Break: Five Ways to Overcome Anxiety and Stress" section of chapter 3, on page 94.)

But even if we say we are only going to evaluate the session after it is over, we may find it is difficult to totally drop assessing our practice while we meditate. In addition to our usual habit of evaluating every moment of experience, we usually meditate with an agenda. Most of us want to meditate "in the right way" because we want to be happy, have less stress, be more focused at work, or take care of our mind. So we compare our practice to our idealized concept of what meditation ought to be like.

In one way, this can't be helped. We all want to be happier, have less stress, or improve our mental edge. But the downside is that we are still caught up in wanting to achieve one thing and avoid another. We are still fully invested in the belief that one set of circumstances—even if they are only mental circumstances—will make us happy, while another set of circumstances will not. We are still in the same endless cycle: scrambling to achieve, prolong, defend, lose, and achieve again, again and again. As we saw previously, that can only lead to brief periods of the kind of happiness that is always suffused with a little tinge of insecurity. But meditation without an agenda has so much more to offer! At first, it may take a little courage to remain present in the face of whatever arises without pushing the ugly stuff away. But soon we discover that we are just fine no matter what thoughts or emotions arise, as long as we stay present and focused on the practice. That is the first glimpse of basic happiness.

In the beginning, it may seem impossible to sit down without the secret hope for a good meditation session. But that's okay! We can simply make the wish at the beginning of the session that we will practice without too much hope or fear, our only agenda being to meditate. Then while we are practicing, whenever we notice we are starting to evaluate, we just respond in exactly the same way as any other time we become distracted: we return to the object, the support for our meditation.

Every moment we remember to place our attention on the breath is a moment of meditation. Every time we notice that we have become distracted, that is meditation. It's really and truly that simple. We don't need to check or evaluate. We just need to do it.

In most kinds of meditation programs, people meditate to reduce stress, become happier or more present. These are worthy goals. But the very intention to reach a goal can in itself become an impediment to enjoying the full benefit of meditation. In fact, as long as we are basing our meditation on a particular set of experiential goals—such as being happier—although we may experience more happiness, it will still be based on the uncertain foundation of temporary circumstances. That means that if circumstances change, so will the benefits of the practice.

Ironically, if a meditation program is promising happiness, less stress, or peace as a fixed goal, although you will probably make some progress toward the goal, the very goal itself is an obstacle. This kind of meditation will perhaps bring us to the pinnacle of the kind of happiness found in passing circumstances, but no further. Authentic meditation is radical because it is free of any goal other than engaging in the practice. Yet, engaging in the practice in this way gives us mastery of our own mind: we can decide where to place our attention and not become distracted. Our minds become so pliable and workable that eventually contentment can be found even in challenging circumstances. By making this radical shift to agendaless meditation, we can become basically happy.

But hey, wait a minute, doesn't wanting to arrive in the present moment mean we have a goal? Well, sure. It is useful to want to be in the present moment; it motivates us to actually make the effort to meditate. But wanting to be in the present moment actually doesn't help us be in the present moment while meditating. In fact, just like any other desire, if we think about it while meditating, it will only carry us away from the present moment. The present moment isn't really a place, yet it's always here—where else *could* it be? We just need to notice what already is the case. So we don't evaluate, we meditate!

All right, but aren't we still concerned with creating circumstances so that we will be in the present? Yes. We use the habitual tendency of the mind to grasp in a way that ends grasping. So, in the beginning meditation is a slightly contrived way to become familiar with remaining present. We use an object, such as the breath, and put our grasping on to the breath, rather than on to whatever thoughts might arise. But as we get more and more used to remaining present, we no longer need a support. The present moment isn't something we create, so the slight contrivance of using an object will eventually become unnescessary. Our own familiarity with being present will be all that we need.

This familiarity is like reading. If we pass a sign on the road, without thinking about it, we read what it says. We are so familiar with reading, that whenever we see something written we read it, without thinking, "Oh, there are some letters; now I need to understand what they mean." In the same way, just noticing that we are aware will naturally bring us into the present moment, the state of non-distraction.

By daring to engage in agendaless meditation, being fully present and open to whatever thoughts or moods arise, you can discover a contentment that you might not have even considered possible. The habit of constantly engaging in comparison and evaluation will naturally relax. At first, that will occur in your meditation practice itself. Yet, gradually you will find that you react to situations with equanimity and humor, no matter what life throws your way. And through all of life's ups and downs, you have greater calmness and stability, because you won't be as bound to circumstances. If you want to meditate to become calm, focused, or lower your blood pressure, that's a valid reason to start meditating.

But amazingly, all these benefits will actually increase when we give up our hope of attaining them! If you would like to reap the full benefits that meditation has to offer, then aspire to let go of any agendas. That aspiration will gradually lead to authentic agendaless meditation. At the beginning of a meditation session, reflect for a few moments on your wish to practice for the practice itself, free from any hope or fear for how it might turn out. It is even good to say it out loud: "I will treat all thoughts the same way, whether they are thoughts about my practice or anything else that passes through my mind. Once I notice the thought, I will let it be and return my attention to the object of my meditation."

The more we cultivate an attitude of gratitude, the easier it will be to engage in agendaless meditation. The more we engage in agendaless meditation, the more likely gratitude will spontaneously arise in our mind instead of the exhausting habit of evaluating and comparing.

CHAPTER 6

Be
Present

I don't know who my grandfather was;
I am much more concerned to know
what his grandson will be.

—Abraham Lincoln

A s we've seen, we can turn our attention toward the present moment through the practice of meditation. While that's a good first step, we have to be able to bring the awareness of the present moment from the meditation seat into ordinary everyday experiences. That is the way we can most effectively go beyond our normal habit of constantly evaluating the quality of our experience.

The whole point of meditation practice is to become so familiar with non-distraction that we can integrate this presence of mind into whatever we're doing. That way, when things are going well, we can drop most of our usual strategies for trying to keep the good times rolling and instead just be present and enjoy. Also, when disaster strikes we won't completely lose our equanimity and become depressed, and we will be better able to do what needs to be done without becoming completely overwhelmed by anxiety. The more we are able to do that, the more basic happiness will arise, even in difficult circumstances.

Since we have already been talking a lot about meditation practice and gratitude, we can now explore how to remind ourselves of an attitude of gratitude and experience being present as we go about our day. So, let's get to it!

INTEGRATING MINDFUL AWARENESS INTO DAILY ACTIVITY

Meditation isn't only about how we are during meditation. Meditation is realized by a shift in how we are during everyday activities. It's wonderful if you can begin each day with the Focus on the Breath or Creating Space exercises. When you start the day this way, even if you can only do a few minutes, it has the potential to transform your day. But often, even if we begin our day with practice, we find that as we step out our door, the events of the day take over and we get completely distracted by them. The awareness of simply being present seems to have completely vanished. So, what is a poor helpless meditator to do?

MINDFUL MINI-BREAK

In order to get used to being fully present, you have to keep remembering during the day to take a short break and watch the breath, create space, or simply appreciate the moment. This is called taking a mindful mini-break because we stop whatever we are doing, we drop whatever we are thinking about, and just be present—stop, drop, and be present.

- Find a moment when you can drop everything—all the looping thoughts and stress. If you really need them, those thoughts will still be there when you get back.

- Spend a few moments on creating space, focusing on the breath or simply appreciating the moment.

A mini-break can be as short as one minute. Try to take as many mindful mini-breaks as you can throughout the day.

THE MINI-BREAK:
FIVE WAYS TO OVERCOME ANXIETY AND STRESS

Perhaps the biggest obstacle to taking a meaningful mindful mini-break is feeling overcome by anxiety and stress. The funny thing is that this is probably when we need a mini-break the most. Here are some tips on how to make a mini-break a mindful one.

1. **Just remembering "meditation" can be enough.** The first few times you take a mini-break, don't expect too much. After all, nearly all of us have been developing the habit of distraction for our entire lives—and Buddhists will tell you it's much longer than that! So, when you take a meditation mini-break you can just think "meditation" and rest your attention on that word for a few moments. This helps establish a habit of taking meditation mini-breaks. After a few times of taking mini-breaks in this way, you can also try the Focusing on the Breath practice or using another object to place your attention upon.

2. **Creating space in every space.** While it can be challenging to practice creating space out in the world, it can be a helpful exercise for any time you start to feel stressed out. You might need to be a little creative though.

· · · · · · · PHAKCHOK RINPOCHE · · · · · · ·

A friend of mine invited me to visit him at his office in midtown Manhattan. I had never been in a big American office building before, and I was really curious to see what it was like. Earlier, my friend said it was impossible in the chaos of the office environment to do the Creating Space exercise. At first, I understood exactly what he meant, since everyone was in a cubicle and there was so much rushing around and no privacy. After a few cups of tea, nature called and he took me to the restroom. I sat in a stall and thought this is the perfect place for a mini-break. No one can bother you here.

· · · · · · · · · · · ·

So, if you are in the office and feeling very frazzled, just go to the bathroom for a few minutes, sit down on the toilet, and create space. In the toilet stall, no one can see you or know what you're doing. Or at least they may think they know and so will leave you to your business, which in this case is creating space.

Likewise, if your boss or coworker starts criticizing you, listen calmly to what she is saying but at the same time look at your mind and try to create space. This also works in your personal life with friends and lovers. You can do this by just recalling how it feels when you are creating space. You won't get as stressed out and upset, so you will be less likely to react straightaway with anger or disturbing emotions. Then it will be easier to address the situation with a calm and clear mind.

3. **Overcome agitation and anxiety by remembering the feeling of peace.** This method involves evoking the memory of an especially peaceful meditation session. In our discussion of "agendaless meditation" (page 86), we explain how to lock down a vivid memory of a meditation session to recall later. When you feel particularly agitated or anxious, try to recall a time when your meditation was especially calm. Think about the room or environment you were in and any special smell or sound you can recall. But most importantly, remember what it felt like. Spend the entire mindful mini-break recalling the peaceful feeling you had during that particular meditation session. Make that peaceful feeling the object of your meditation.

4. **Cultivate an attitude of gratitude.** As we said earlier, when the habit of distraction kicks in, we get carried away by judgments and looping thoughts. The best way to overcome this is by focusing on gratitude and appreciation. During your mindful mini-break you can recall something in your life that you appreciate. It is even easier to think of something if you spent a few minutes on gratitude in the morning. You can simply return to your morning thought of gratitude.

5. When all else fails, use the anxiety as the object. Sometimes, we are so completely overwhelmed by anxiety that it seems like nothing will work. The danger here is we can add to our agitation or anxiety simply by becoming frustrated that we can't seem to do anything about it. Instead of trying to make it go away, we can just use the feeling of anxiety as the focus of our meditation mini-break.

Ask yourself, how do I know that I am anxious? Is it a sensation, a feeling in my body? Or a tone of voice in my internal dialogue? Or a particular kind of thought that keeps churning in my mind? Or an image of something that I am worried about?

You don't need to indulge in running commentaries such as "I wish I didn't feel so anxious" or "I wish the meditation practice would work!" Instead just allow yourself to focus, without any distraction, on the feeling of anxiety or agitation, seeing if it is a thought, an emotion, a sensation in your body, or maybe some combination of those. Try as precisely as possible to identify what it is you're referring to as an "anxious feeling." Don't get into how you feel about it or how you would rather feel or any other kinds of judgments. In that way, even anxiety can bring you into the present moment.

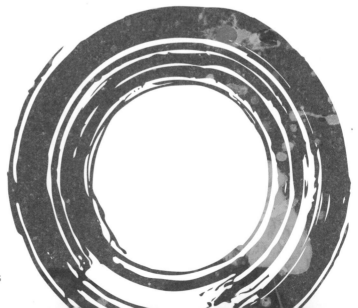

Nothing can bring
you peace but yourself.

—Ralph Waldo Emerson

DEVELOPING THE MINI-BREAK HABIT: USING TRIGGERS

Even though we may want to take meditation mini-breaks throughout the day, often we get so caught up in our daily routine that we simply forget to stop, drop, and be present. Therefore, we need a way to remind ourselves to take a mindful mini-break. So, we pick specific common events that will prompt us to take a moment to stop and take a break. Then when we encounter these reminders, we take a few minutes to rest in meditation, create space, or cultivate gratitude. We call these reminders triggers, because they can quickly click us into taking a mini-break.

1. **Pick a mini-break trigger**. During the day, there will be lots of meditation mini-break possibilities. For example, if you ride on the bus or subway, you can take a few moments to watch the breath or use the sound of the train as a support.

   We are often waiting for something—a bus, friends to show up, or one of those interminable customer-service call holds. Instead of becoming bored, lost in a daydream, or distracted by e-mail or a game on our phone, we can watch the breath. Even the checkout line at the market can be a chance to use a physical sensation or another support for coming into the present moment.

   If you work in an office, your trigger could be when a meeting ends early: when you get back to your desk, instead of immediately diving into your e-mail, try focusing on the breath for sixty seconds.

Where I used to work, a lunch truck would come around 11:45 each day and honk its horn. While most of the office ran out to get a sandwich or a taco, I would seize the moment for a meditation mini-break. The office would suddenly be quiet, and I would sit in my cubicle and focus on my breath or creating space. Since it usually took fifteen to twenty minutes for everyone to get their lunch, I would saunter out after a few minutes and still get my taco. And, man, those tacos were good. And they were made even better coming at the end of a spacious break.

. . . .

Whatever you decide to pick as a trigger, the main point is that it should be something that will remind you to stop, drop, and be present. Take a few moments to imagine what your trigger (or triggers) might be.

2. **Mentally plan for your trigger.** At the start of your day (the best time is at the end of a morning meditation session—you are meditating in the morning, right?), take a few moments to imagine your trigger and what you will do. Go over it a few times in your mind: visualize where you might be when you encounter the trigger or what the circumstances will be.

Imagine how you will take a meditation mini-break and what the break will be like, how it will feel to take a few minutes just to meditate in the middle of the day. Strongly make the wish that every time you see, feel, or hear your meditation trigger you will remember to take your mini-break.

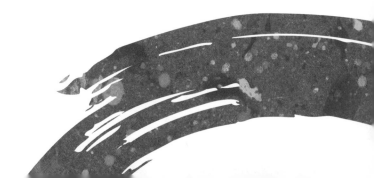

3. **Set a target, count the mini-breaks.** Having goals is an important part of life. Our life is filled with goals, from meeting a good friend for lunch to planning what to get for dinner or saving for a vacation, we spend most of our life making plans and working toward enacting those plans or goals. Each day you can set a target number of mini-breaks you want to take. Here is some step-by-step advice on how to set realistic meditation mini-break goals:

- Make the daily goal achievable. In the beginning, if you set a goal that is too ambitious you might quickly lose heart. Start with setting a modest goal—perhaps three times a day, but even once is good.

- Count each time you take a mini-break.

- In the evening write down the number of mini-breaks you took and set the goal for the next day. If you are badly missing your goal each day you should consider lowering your total. For example, if you plan to do thirty mini-breaks each day and are only doing three, maybe you need to reset.

- Slowly increase the number of mini-breaks per day. If you did three times per day last week (or month), increase the goal to four per day.

- Set a goal and start counting.

People often ask us how many mini-breaks they should take during the day. The answer is take as many as you can but not so many that it makes you feel pressured. Mini-breaks need to be exactly that: a break from the normal distraction and stress of our day. So, work up to a good number slowly. Start with one mini-break per day and then add more and more until it feels like the right number.

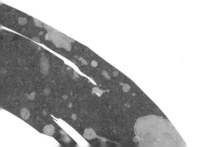

NEVER BE BORED AGAIN!

When we tell people that meditation is an antidote to boredom, they often look at us wide-eyed as if we have gone off the deep end. After all, isn't it true that one of the biggest obstacles to meditation is that sitting and doing nothing is the very definition of booooorrrrrring? What is so exciting about watching the breath?

For most people, the very idea of being bored or left for a few moments with nothing to do is almost unbearable. Today's wired society has exacerbated this phenomenon. Most of us carry a smartphone in our pocket with instant access to social media, the Internet, music, YouTube videos—an infinite variety of entertainment options, just a click away. On the one hand, most people complain about the relentlessly stressful, fast pace of daily life; on the other hand, they have designed their lives so they never lack entertainment options. We now have more stuff happening more of the time.

Remember we said that we were going to have some fun? This is a chance to play with your mind and see what is really going on. Next time you are meditating and the "this is really boring" thought arises or the "I hope the buzzer signaling meditation is over rings soon" thought comes, that's where the fun begins. Does it seem a little uncomfortable to just have to sit there for a little bit more? Why? It's not as if someone is sticking a hot needle into your eye. At that moment, ask yourself, what is the source of my discomfort? Is it the thought itself that creates a bit of anxiousness or is there something inherently awful about just sitting quietly? And if it is the thought, how can a few words floating through your mind have so much power? Are you really going to be

trapped by always habitually reacting to thoughts instead of just being in non-distraction?

Why is this fun? Because we get to go beyond just habitually responding to thoughts and emotions and instead become a curious "mind-explorer." This mind-exploration is intellectually satisfying, and what a relief it is not to be held hostage by our habits.

Even if this approach to meditation isn't so boring, we can still wonder, how can meditation be an antidote to boredom? And the answer is: **whenever there is a dull moment, use it to meditate.**

Normally we spend a lot of our time waiting for things to happen. We wait for the train to arrive, the laundry to finish, or the meeting to start. Or it could be that we get stuck at a café waiting for a friend or arrive at the movies a bit too early. Instead of whipping out your smartphone, just notice your breath. By focusing our attention lightly on our breath, we bring mindfulness into our awareness and enter into non-distraction. Now you have a productive and interesting way to pass through those moments where you used to get bored. So, there: meditation *is* an antidote to boredom.

BUILDING A DAILY MEDITATION PRACTICE

Nearly everybody struggles with establishing a regular daily meditation practice. It's a lot like a New Year's resolution to get regular exercise at the gym. At first, we are there everyday, but then after a while life just seems to take over. The key to establishing a daily practice is to cultivate enthusiasm and consistency.

CULTIVATING ENTHUSIASM

Enthusiasm means cultivating a positive attitude toward being fully present in the moment. By contemplating the benefits of creating space, an attitude of gratitude, and meditation, the enthusiasm for learning to be fully present and undistracted will naturally follow. Even so, we all need a good strategy to create a habit of consistent practice.

* * * * * * * * PHAKCHOK RINPOCHE * * * * * * * *

I have always been the kind of person who naturally rebels against any kind of system or obligation. For much of my life, when I heard the instructions we're going over in this section, I would immediately try to do the opposite. To overcome this tendency, I have had to accept that this contrariness is a natural part of my character. I can only do things if I feel I really understand the benefit.

So I studied the reasons for meditation and tried to see if they added up. The logic explained earlier in the book about the downfalls of distraction and the benefits of non-distraction began to make sense, not just intellectually but in my own experience. I saw how my mind was when I was meditating regularly, and how my mind was when I skipped a bunch of days. I was surprised to see that when I meditated regularly, I was calmer, more content, and better able to deal with unexpected challenges. When I didn't meditate, I was more reactive and had more negative emotions.

Because I am quite stubborn and headstrong, it took a few years before this kind of reflection fully convinced me. Even now I have to regularly remind myself about the benefits of being fully present. But it is through this that I find the motivation to practice every day.

* * * * * * * * * * *

This book is filled with lots of reasons for becoming more and more familiar with present-moment awareness. It is good to highlight things that speak to you and go over them again and again. In this way, you will naturally become more and more enthusiastic about the practice.

But the key point is to make this fun, not a chore. For example, you could make a canned Google search that aggregates meditation news. Or configure an app on your smartphone to collect meditation news items (there are lots of popular apps that do this). If you have a friend who is also learning meditation, meet regularly for lunch to compare notes. Most importantly, remember to celebrate and appreciate the effort you are making.

CONSISTENCY

Even if we do generate enthusiasm, we may start with the best of intentions, but life seems to somehow intervene, and suddenly we may realize that a week or two has gone by and our enthusiasm has completely evaporated. We just aren't meditating all that much, again! Arrrrrgh.

Back in the day, when I was first getting into meditation, I would make all kinds of promises to myself that I would meditate every day for a really long time. Often this would be right after attending an inspiring meditation lecture. Filled with enthusiasm, I had big plans. It would work for a while, and then slowly I would meditate for shorter amounts of time or skip a day here and there until finally my practice was no longer daily and, when I did find the time to meditate, I was pretty restless the entire time.

Recognizing there was a difference between how much meditation I would like to do and how much I was able to do was an important step. I was behaving like I was in a sprint but in fact I was running in a marathon so long that it could last my entire life. This lifelong marathon clearly called for a different approach. Then, I began by making a commitment to myself (again) that I would meditate every day, but instead of promising to do it for the rest of my life I would vow to do it for a certain number of days. I also committed to a certain number of minutes that I was sure I could do each day no matter what. If I had more time or was inspired, I might do more, but I never dropped below my minimum.

What was my minimum? Two minutes. How many days did I promise to do my measly two minutes for? Three days.

Two minutes a day for three days. There isn't anyone who couldn't do that. Yup, even I could do that much. At the end of three days I made a new commitment, another two minutes for three days. Slowly I built it up. Soon I was committing to three minutes every day for four days. Then five minutes a day. And so on. I increased the amount slowly. After a while I didn't need to commit to a certain number of days. It had been many months and I was meditating every day. This habit continued to grow even after I worked insanely long hours at my Silicon Valley job. Now I don't have to think that much about it. It took years, but I never miss a day anymore, and I don't feel completely satisfied until I have done my minimum each day.

· · · · · · · · · · ·

It's a good plan, then, to start with an achievable number of minutes of meditation that we promise to do no matter what. Although the time of day can vary, most of the greatest meditators through the centuries have recommended meditating first thing in the morning. So, for example, we could commit to three minutes a day for three days and then, to make sure we have time, set the alarm to wake up five minutes early. We won't miss the five minutes of sleep, and we can use the extra time to do our three minutes.

Now, we have a commitment to meditation and some extra time in our day to do it! Gradually we can increase both the number of minutes we commit to meditate and how many days that commitment will last.

If you find the length of time you have committed to is a bit of a stretch, at the end of your committed number of days you can lower the number of minutes. That's why it is good, especially in the beginning, to commit to your daily practice only for a short number of days (three to five) at a time. Then at the end of the period, you can renew your pledge. Strengthening the habit of making a promise to yourself that you can actually keep builds positive momentum toward a lifelong meditation practice.

A DAILY PLAN FOR BASIC HAPPINESS

We've concluded the basic happiness section, so let's try to bring everything we've discussed together into a formula for daily practice. What we are suggesting is something to spark your imagination and inspire you to try to go for it. This isn't supposed to be another burden to carry around. In the beginning, doing everything listed below will likely be too much. But with a little practice, you can easily integrate these exercises into the life you already have. We have tried this out on lots of ~~victims~~ friends, including ourselves, and it has helped a lot of people experience basic happiness. So play around, see what works. Make basic happiness your own, and maybe enjoy life a little bit more.

By taking just thirty minutes out of your day, the taste of basic happiness will be yours. You can do more, and less is also okay. It's important to try to keep these practices almost every day, even if you can only manage a few minutes. But it's more important to make this fun and not a chore; it's time to be radically happy, after all.

····· BASIC HAPPINESS ·····

MORNING

Wake into the present moment. Instead of jumping out of bed, notice how your body feels by doing a brief body scan; imagine how you will begin the day with meditation practice. Make an aspiration that the day will be one of mindful awareness.

·

Morning meditation. Practice creating space, then meditate for a few minutes using focus on the breath or another method. Spend a few moments reflecting on something you are grateful for. Celebrate and appreciate the effort you made to meditate

·

Mindful drinking. Sip your morning coffee or tea with present-moment awareness.

AFTERNOON

Mindful mini-breaks. Whenever and wherever you can throughout the day, create space, watch your breath, and cultivate an attitude of gratitude.

EVENING

Evening meditation. Take a few moments at the end of the day. Create space and, if you aren't too exhausted, watch the breath for a few minutes. Think of something for tomorrow's gratitude contemplation.

Reflect on how, despite a lifetime spent mostly chasing distraction, you spent a bit of time practicing.

·

Celebrate. Celebrate the few moments you meditated, especially if you took a mini-break or three during the day. Then visualize yourself doing it again tomorrow. Have fun!

·

Mindfully slip into sleep. As you lie in bed, create an attitude of gratitude and then rest as you fall mindfully to sleep.

PART TWO

INTERCONNECTED HAPPINESS

Mastering
your
Heart

nterconnected happiness arises through our interaction with other people. As we saw when we looked at how we go about trying to be happy, when it comes to our day-to-day interactions we sometimes (and maybe even often) behave in ways that are out of accord with our beliefs. We all understand that our environment and the animals, plants, and humans that live in it are interdependently connected to one another. This seamless web of interdependence is fundamental to our scientific understanding of the biosphere. Yet, if we carefully examine our day-to-day activities, we will see that we live out of accord with this understanding. And that keeps us from experiencing interconnected happiness.

THE THREE KEYS TO INTERCONNECTED HAPPINESSS

1. Contemplate the interdependent nature of reality.

Most of us live our lives as if we are discrete entities, clearly distinguishable from the world we find ourselves in. But upon closer examination, we find we are the result of our interconnections with others and our environment. Many of our values, decisions, and habitual ways of thinking—the essence of what we think defines us—are in fact the product of interdependencies. Our culture, the way we are raised, whom we hang with, even the microorganisms in our gut have an impact on how we experience things. Living as if we are completely separable from the world we find ourselves in distorts every aspect of our experience. If we truly contemplate how we're all interconnected, it leads to a counterintuitive switcheroo: we usually think that to properly take care of ourselves and our loved ones, we have to put our needs and theirs before all others. But interconnected happiness arises through cultivating loving-kindness and compassion and by learning to value others in much the same way we value ourselves. In fact, responding to others' needs is also a way for us to nurture our own basic need for happiness and social connection.

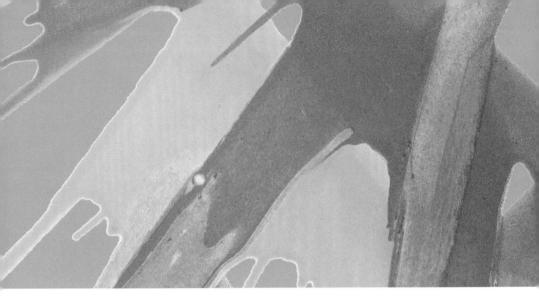

2. Relax the judging.

We make very strong judgments about people a few seconds after meeting them, yet these judgments are often incorrect and difficult to change. This judgmental habit prevents us from truly seeing others, making good decisions, and authentically experiencing the world around us. Here we learn how to relax this habit of making quick judgments through cultivating loving-kindness and compassion during meditation, as well as learning to celebrate the good fortune of others.

3. Be attentive.

Interconnected happiness arises through our daily interactions with other people. And that is what the slogan *Be attentive* is all about. We can harness the insights and warmth gained in the previous two sections to gradually shift the way we experience others, even really difficult people, and learn to be satisfied and content without waiting for the whole world to conform to what we think we need.

CHAPTER 7

Contemplate the Interdependent Nature of Reality

When I was around ten, I used to think a lot about how I would use time travel. My interest came after hearing family stories about the great hardship my mother's parents and grandparents went through in Russia during the early years of the twentieth century. My grandmother was still a young girl when her village was burned by white Russians or Cossacks, and the family endured an arduous journey, first on foot to France and then by boat to the United States. My grandfather's family escaped village pogroms by smuggling themselves into St. Petersburg, nearly getting my grandfather and his little brother impaled on pitchforks in the process. There are rumors that as a young teen Grandpa passed out flyers for Trotsky. Anyway, they eventually had to leave St. Petersburg too. I loved science fiction and watched a show called *The Time Tunnel*, where each episode involved using the time tunnel to go back in time.

So I indulged myself in a few fantasies about what I would do with the time tunnel. For one thing, I thought that I could somehow stop Grandma's village from being destroyed by bringing them a few modern weapons. But most of my time was spent thinking about how to help the Trotskyites. I was pretty sure that Trotsky wouldn't have been the horror Stalin was and would have been nice to Russian Jewish families. Furthermore, at this tweener age I was convinced that Trotsky would have allowed democratic institutions to be established.

As it turned out, I had to conclude that there was no way to change the course of history *and* ensure that my grandparents would meet. Even if I could think how to maybe arrange that, how would I get my parents to meet too? And if they didn't meet, I wouldn't exist. And then there was the problem of growing up in Russia. Would that Russian kid still be me? Was I willing to sacrifice my life and most likely my parents for the good of millions? Not only Russians but the whole Cold War in my mind would have been avoided. It was lot to think about.

· · · · · · · · · · ·

Nearly every movie and TV show about time travel demonstrates how hard it is to not mess things up in the present by changing something in the past, no matter how innocuous the change may seem. This is because everything and everyone is connected; everything that happens is based on prior events. This seems pretty obvious; nothing in the universe comes into being without a cause. And every cause or action has an effect. Change one small thing and a whole bunch of other things change too, and over the course of enough time, the effect is nearly limitless.

Everything is interdependent. Nothing exists without being dependent on causes and conditions. Based on causes and conditions, we are born, galaxies arise, atoms form. By the same token, other causes and conditions lead to our passing, great galaxies are no more, and atoms fissure. When we are self-absorbed, we are exaggerating our separateness, making a big deal out of decisions that are often just conditioned responses. We think making choices represents our freedom, but it could actually be reinforcing our slavery.

THE FREEDOM OF CHOICE?

Every day we make decisions, from super important, potentially life-changing decisions to many more that are pretty mundane. We may even pride ourselves on our decision-making abilities, perhaps thinking this ability is what "separates us from the pack." But most decisions are in reality a reflection of the pack. In other words, our decisions are usually the result of our conditioning, our biology, and the group of people we identify most closely with, rather than a completely unique expression of our individuality.

Let's consider a fairly ordinary example and take a look at what it means to choose a bottle at our local wine shop.

For starters, how did that bottle get there? The person who runs the shop had to decide the bottle was sellable. That usually depends in part on at least one well-regarded wine critic praising that particular wine or the person who made the wine, the brand (château), or (if the grapes were purchased from the grower) the vineyard itself. Sometimes, the shop's wine buyer simply liked the taste.

But all of these factors depended on a great deal of other factors, such as the fact that we live on a planet that supports both plant and animal life and that grapes and people were the product of evolution. Quite a few fortunate coincidences needed to occur in order for people and grapes to come into being. Then human beings needed to discover fermentation, and, of course, there was the further discovery that fermented liquids brought on the pleasant feeling of being slightly inebriated. But even more important was the fact that someone noticed that these liquids were often safer to drink than water. Over time, people became better and better at making fermented grapes taste more and more delicious. All kinds of agricultural and mechanical innovations had to take place, and these depended on a series of unrelated events such as the invention of gears and the replacement of ox and plow with gas-powered tractors. Roads were built that facilitated transportation and commerce.

None of these innovations were directly linked to making better-tasting wine, yet they were all part of a bigger interconnected picture. The more you look at all the different dependencies and interdependencies, the more you realize that all of the developments of humanity, if not the entire universe, are somehow connected to the arrival of the particular bottle of wine we chose to enjoy with our friends. So much so that the actual act of choosing a particular wine—a decision we may be very proud of—is the smallest, most insignificant part of the whole chain of events. It is hardly *our* choice at all.

Choosing a bottle of wine is not the only way in which we think we are making a unique, independent decision when we are really being governed by our connections. Most of the actions we take are a habitual response to the cultural, social, and environmental conditions around us.

In an experiment dubbed "The Cookie Monster," researchers studied groups of three random people who go to the same university.[1] In each group, one person was randomly selected to be the leader, and the groups were tasked with a pretty boring project, working on some policy decisions the campus is facing. After twenty minutes, someone arrives with a plate of four cookies. In almost every case the person who was assigned to be group leader (a mere twenty minutes earlier) ends up with the extra cookie. Usually no one says, "Hey, let's divide that extra cookie into three pieces," nor does one of the two nonleaders reach out to take the cookie him- or herself. The extra cookie usually arrives into the mouth of the head honcho.

Why should we be making a big deal out of choices and extra cookies? After all, at least we get a bottle of yummy wine and a cookie. We're pounding away at this point because these examples illustrate that a lot of what we attribute to free will and being "our decisions" are actually just manifestations of the interdependent nature of reality. Our interconnectedness with our environment, other people, and circumstances has a lot to do with why we act the way we do and what choices we make. And as we can see through the lens of Erric's imagined time machine, the choices and decisions of people who seemingly have no connection with us at all, and died years ago, can have an impact on us right now.

This invites us to ask ourselves a question: Do we live in accord with the interdependent nature of reality, what we refer to as "interconnectedness," or is the way we live actually denying it? And if we are denying our interconnectedness, what does that cost us? Another way to put this is: Do you want to be a slave to an unconscious conditioned response to people and things, or is there a more authentic way to interact with this constant dance of interconnectedness? And is there an upside to freeing the slave?

"Happiness is love. Full stop." That is the conclusion of George Vaillant, the director of a seventy-five-year study conducted by Harvard University that followed 268 men over the course of their lives.[2] Vaillant summarized the study's conclusion as the "warmth of relationships throughout life have the greatest positive impact on 'life satisfaction.'" People who enjoyed warm relationships during their lives were much more likely to consider life a success. Here are some of the findings:

They lived longer.

They made considerably more money,
while IQ beyond mediocre had no effect on earnings.

They had better marriages.

They were much more likely to find satisfaction in life.

Growing old with grace and vitality has more to do with
how we live our lives than with our genetic makeup.

Love, really? That's the solution? Perhaps you're thinking we've gone soft. Okay, so let's be practical about it. Rather than focus on a big abstract thing, like love, let's think simply in terms of the kind of warm relationships mentioned on the previous page. We feel someone is warm toward us when he or she acts in a kind and caring manner, don't we? So perhaps that's the point, not some kind of airy-fairy notions of love but basic human kindness and care, which you can do anywhere.

· · · · · · · · ERRIC SOLOMON · · · · · · · ·

During the first dot-com boom, which started in the late 1990s, companies in Silicon Valley were dealing with staff turnover of at least 35 percent per year. It was almost as though anyone who could fog a mirror was able to go out and get a job that paid way more than they were currently earning. Trying to manage projects in that kind of atmosphere was quite a challenge. Quickly it dawned on those of us who were leading companies that we were managing volunteers, rather than employees, since everyone who wanted to get another job could do so with seemingly little more effort than a finger snap. Where I was working at this time, the human resources department figured out which teams had better-than-average retention and interviewed employees to see if they could identify a trend that would account for a higher retention rate.

A few departments had performed extremely well, with less than 10 percent yearly turnover. Employees on these teams talked about their manager very differently than employees did in many other departments. It turned out the biggest factor in determining whether someone was likely to stay was the relationship the person had with management. In low-turnover groups people said things like, "My manager is interested in me, in how well I am in my job, not just whether we are making deadlines or not." Furthermore, departments that had lower turnover had managers who were more likely to use constructive criticism as feedback.

In high-turnover teams, the manager may have been well liked, but people said things such as, "My manager only gives me the good news about how I am doing but never where my shortcomings lie or what we need to do about them." And perhaps this kind of approach to managing was happening more than ever. Well-intentioned managers were afraid to say anything negative that might lead an employee to quit. However, in the low-turnover teams people said things like, "My manager gives it to me straight, not only what I am doing well but where I can improve. But not only that, she works with me to come up with a plan to help me excel. This is what I need to grow in my career: a manager who cares enough about me to tell me the bad news as well as the good."

Being kind doesn't mean just being a wimp. It means taking your caring far enough that you're willing to be brave enough to give it to someone straight. And also to engage with others to help them flourish. Who wins? Well, according to the Harvard study, the kind and caring person. The more open, kind, and caring we are, the better off we are, and maybe even everyone else as well. Like a disease, it spreads. Except that unlike a disease, we are all healthier having caught the bug.

In the previous part on basic happiness, we talked a lot about the benefits of the present moment. When we are fully present, we are better able to enjoy the good times, whenever they arrive. In non-distraction, Erric can enjoy his time on the beach free from useless "Too bad every day can't be like this" thoughts. Basic happiness is the kind of contentment that comes from enjoyment, the fruit of non-distraction. But interconnected happiness is a little different: it's the kind of satisfaction that comes from *finding meaning or purpose in our lives*. And what does this meaning or purpose arise from?

That is the big ah-ha in the Harvard study. "Warm relations" lead to feelings that one's life has meaning and a sense of satisfaction with life. Cultivating interconnected happiness doesn't have to be a big deal—putting a smile on someone's face when you pour them a cup of coffee at a diner, helping a disabled person onto the bus, or just generally being kind—all these things add up. And that eventually leads to life satisfaction.

It's pretty easy to see a glimpse of how this might work in your own life. Think of a time in the last month when you helped someone for no other reason than because you saw a need. When you recall this moment, don't you get a little bit of a warm feeling inside?

• • • • • • • • • •

The Nepalese earthquake occurred in the middle of the monsoon season, on Saturday, April 25, 2015, at 11:56 a.m., with its epicenter approximately fifty miles northwest of Kathmandu. This initial quake lasted approximately fifty seconds. There is some disagreement about the magnitude, 7.8 or 8.1. All I know is that it was far stronger than anything I could have imagined, and those fifty seconds were the longest seconds of my life. Immediately, in less than a minute, our world was turned upside down. Buildings were destroyed or so badly damaged that it was unsafe to be inside them; we had more than forty-five aftershocks ranging in strength from 4.5 to 6.6. Like nearly everyone else, my wife, two very young children, and I spent the next two months living outside in a tent.

Initially we were in a small one-person camping tent where four of us slept like sardines. When the rains started seeping through, we had to use our shoes as a kind of improvised dam against the stream of water trying to enter our tent. My parents were living right next to us, also in a very small tent, which was not as modern as ours. Behind their tent was the young boy who is the reincarnation of my grandfather. We used makeshift toilets, dug out of the ground with plastic wrapped around the hole. We were some of the lucky ones, since we at least had a bit of shelter from the torrential rain. My father's health can be a little fragile, so in this situation I was quite concerned about him. We went without showering for some time, my kids got head lice, and we were eating mostly rice and lentils. Honestly, it was hard to ever completely relax because of the constant shaking from the aftershocks.

The afternoon of the earthquake we were mostly in a state of shock and were literally counting aftershocks. The first indicator of an aftershock was the dogs barking, the birds flying, followed by the humans shouting! In the confusion, we could barely find the presence of mind to look to make sure our many neighbors, family, and friends were safe. The next morning, I went around the monastery compound to see if all the monks in their makeshift tents were comfortable and to assess the damage to the monastery caused by the earthquake.

The monks were shaken but intact, but our monastery—which was built by my grandfather, grandmother, uncle, and father, along with our senior monks and students—was badly hit and had incurred major structural damage. It was truly heartbreaking, but because of all the blessings, our monastery, which was built in the old-fashioned style with no iron beams, was still holding up—sitting upright like an old dignified meditation master. Just when I stepped outside and into the courtyard, one of our younger monks came walking toward me and dropped into my arms crying. His mother had died when her house collapsed in a nearby village, and that moment shook me out of my own self-absorbed concerns.

No one was immune to a situation like this, and so instead of waiting for help to come, we all had to take matters into our own hands. Our monastery needed to organize a relief effort. My wife and I joined in and helped to bring food, medicine, and shelter to surrounding villages almost nonstop for the next two months. It was a struggle to be both a survivor and to find the inner strength and presence of mind to constantly be there for those in need.

Strangely, when I think back to that time, while I do remember the suffering, my most vivid memories are quite different. I remember little things. I remember my wife's sense of humor—the way she teased me about how much better organized nearby Shechen Monastery was than ours, especially when they came around first thing in the morning to offer hot tea for everyone camped outside. I remember the faces of the villagers when we handed them tarps to sleep under and to shelter them from the rain. I remember how kind and considerate our group of monks and nuns were, not only to all the people we helped but toward each other. But mostly I remember the quiet satisfaction that came from being part of a team that was making at least a small dent in the devastation.

It wasn't an easy time—there was sadness and heartbreak, frustration and despair—but there was always something positive that needed to be done, that could be done, and really no time to dwell on anything else. Even though I am what people might call "a member of the clergy," and my job is to respond to people in need, I never faced such a challenge before, nor was I ever so inspired to do something. All of us who were there were victims and caregivers. All of Nepal, it seemed, was connected—depending on one another just to make it through another day. When I look back now on that time, although I was surrounded by tragedy, it was also a time of joy. There was a lot of satisfaction to be had just by being able to provide for those in great need.

· · · · · · · · · · ·

When we are more focused on others' needs, we find meaning in our lives. But, when we are preoccupied with ourselves, we tend to be working against the natural interconnectedness that is a fundamental quality of the universe.

Our proposition is this: the more we can live in accord with the natural interconnectedness with others and our environment, the more likely we are to make decisions and choices that arise from our own natural intelligence and less from our culturally conditioned or habitual way of acting and reacting.

Habitual reactions, when left unexamined, seem like choices we are making. But those aren't actually choices made from our own authentic wisdom (i.e., freedom). They are just culturally or biologically conditioned ways of responding (i.e., slavery). The more we recognize that every little act, even buying a bottle of wine, is not the achievement of one little walled-off person but rather the act of someone connected to others in a warm embrace—and the more we are in touch with our own core of warmheartedness—the better off we are, and the better off our friends and colleagues are.

DEEPENING YOUR SENSE OF INTERCONNECTEDNESS

When you can strengthen your sense of being always connected to others, it will make it that much easier for you to live your life informed by kindness and caring—and interconnected happiness, of course. Before we go into how to get in touch with our natural capacity for warmheartedness and bring it into nearly any situation, it will be helpful to try out a few exercises. The goal of the following exercises is twofold: remembering interconnectedness and then acknowledging the kindness and caring that has touched you.

First, in order to experience interconnected happiness, it helps to see the interconnectedness of everything, rather than focus on separateness. Interconnectedness is a fundamental aspect of reality, and when we live our lives out of harmony with reality, it affects how we view everything in our life. Seeing through the blurred lens of separateness, we risk acting and reacting based on a false set of assumptions. When we focus on separateness, we are basing our worldview on bad data, like diving headfirst into a swimming pool without checking if there is any water in it.

Second, we need to investigate the kindness and caring in our lives. It is only through the kindness and care of others that we are even here. We survived infancy, we learned stuff, we have a livelihood—all of this is a result of interconnectedness and the kindness of others. We don't know all of those who have helped us; we can never know all of the people who've made it possible for us to live and flourish. Like Blanche DuBois in *A Streetcar Named Desire*, we "have always depended on the kindness of strangers."

It is also true that we have all suffered traumas and defeats, and we shouldn't push those away. We need to acknowledge them and learn from them. But too often we allow the worst of life's setbacks to reinforce our sense of separateness and despair. One way to heal that feeling of being isolated is through focusing on all the kindness and care we have received in life.[3] But the important thing is to begin to acknowledge and reexperience the kindnesses and love we have received. It will make it so much easier for us to be kind, considerate, and discerning, rather than judgmental, in our daily interactions. These are the fruits of recognizing our interconnectedness.

We're going to ask you to think about everyday occurrences and spend a bit of time reflecting on all the different events that had to occur for them to happen. In other words, you will remind yourself again and again to see interconnectedness in the context of your daily life.

EXERCISE 13

INTERCONNECTEDNESS ON THE TABLE

- Take a few moments to reflect on the food sitting on the plate in front of you.

- Imagine all the different people who helped to bring this food to your table. The staff at the store where you bought it, the farmer who grew it, the trucker who delivered it.

- Then consider how those people got there. Who taught the farmer? Who raised the trucker? Who built the truck? How did we get trucks in the first place? How about the road the truck traveled on? Who built it? And so on. See how far you can go.

INTERCONNECTEDNESS AT WORK

Whatever you do for a living, think for a moment about all the people who are connected to your job—your coworkers, the people who buy the goods or pay for the services you provide. If you sit in an office, who made your desk and chair? Who designed the building? Who constructed it? How did the materials get there? How did people learn to make office buildings anyway?

CONTEMPLATING KINDNESS

In part one on basic happiness, we explained how to develop an attitude of gratitude. Here we will extend that practice even further by contemplating the kindness of everyday objects and taking a deeper look at the people who have shown us kindness.

THE KINDNESS OF THINGS

Are there things you use every day that make your life easier? How would your life be without a refrigerator? Indoor plumbing? Maybe the phone you use to surf the web? This exercise is a little bit like the gratitude exercise Appreciating a Quality or Possession (page 83), except we thank *the object* for its kindness. Kindness? Yes. For example, the fridge is kindly keeping our food bacteria free, which protects our health. The plants in our house or yard generously produce oxygen, which helps us breathe.

Kindness isn't always the result of a conscious act. When we look at a beautiful flower, just appreciating the beauty of the flower brings us into the present moment. That is due to the kindness of the flower. Gazing at the flower's fresh beauty brings us joy—a kind gift from the flower. Too often people say things like, "it's a cold cruel world," and it is true that bad things sometimes happen. But that can't be the sole definition of our universe, because it is also a world brimming with natural, spontaneous kindness.

- In the morning do five to ten minutes of creating space.

- Think of an object you use daily, or almost daily, whose utility is invaluable. Think about how that object is part of the kindness of interconnectedness, and feel gratitude as before.

- By extension, think of the kindness of all the people who made the object of gratitude. Because if the object is a kindness, the people who made it are also part of that.

- Now you can relax your mind, letting go of the thought experiment you were doing. For a few minutes, rest in meditation by focusing on the breath or using any of the other methods we discussed earlier.

REMEMBERING THE KINDNESS WE'VE RECEIVED

In spite of all that we have had to endure, our lives have been and continue to be shaped by the kindness and care of others. When we were too young to feed ourselves, someone fed us, put us under a warm blanket at night, and brought us to a doctor when we were too ill to climb down from our crib. During our school years, some of us had mentors, people who taught us valuable stuff or at least how to graduate. Perhaps it was a spiritual mentor who introduced us to our religious or spiritual beliefs. Each day, we continue to have people in our lives who show us kindness and care. It could be someone who shows us the ropes at work or brings us chicken soup when we have the flu. It could be someone who offered us a kindness as small as asking what floor we're going to on the elevator or giving us directions when our GPS seems to be wrong.

Usually, when we first try to think of people who supported us, our mind seemingly goes in the opposite direction. We immediately can recall every slight—small or devastatingly big—that we have had to endure. With a little practice, we can gradually think of all kinds of people who touched our lives. Maybe some of the memories that surface hadn't been relived in ages, yet, with a little effort, they revealed themselves.

Make a list of everyone who has offered you kindess or care. Whenever you think of it, add a new name to your list. They needn't be perfect saints with impeccable motivation. They just need to have shown you some care and kindness.

- In your morning meditation, start by creating space.

- Recall one of the people on your list. As you think of what that person gave you, remember to honor the memory with appreciation and gratitude.

- In the beginning, it may be helpful to consider someone who cared for you when you were quite young. Allow yourself to feel that person's love and care, nurturing you as a child. Feel appreciation for that person's kindess.

- At the end of every session, rest for a few minutes by focusing on the breath or using one of the other ways of meditating we discussed earlier.

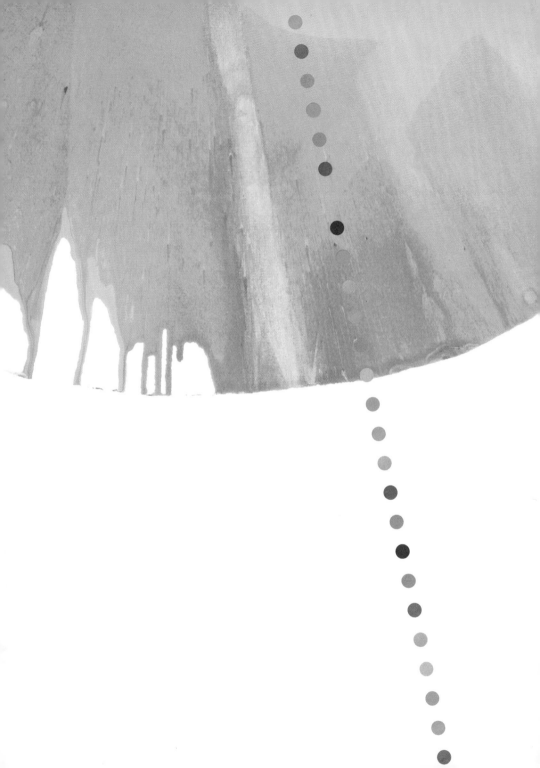

RESTING IN THE LIGHT OF KINDNESS

After trying the previous exercise out for a few weeks, expand your imagination to include not just the people who cared for you but the people who cared for the people who cared for you. Our lives are supported by innumerable kindnesses that go back generation upon generation. It doesn't matter if you knew these people. Just know that they are there and consider their contribution.

- In your morning meditation, start by creating space.

- Imagine the people who have offered you kindess or care as part of a chain or web that goes on and on—the carers of the carers, almost into infinity. It's an unending lattice of support—kindness and care and gratitude and appreciation.

- You can imagine everyone as bathed in the warm light of loving joy, all these people interconnected by kindness. Imagine not only what it looks like but also how it feels.

- Recognize that although you have suffered setbacks and trauma in your life, you are here because of kindness and care.

- At the end of every session, rest for a few minutes by focusing on the breath or using one of the other ways of meditating we discussed earlier.

Everything can be taken from a man [*sic*]
but one thing: the last of the human freedoms—
to choose one's attitude in any given set of
circumstances, to choose one's own way.

—Viktor Frankl, *Man's Search for Meaning*

We normally think having choices and the ability to choose *is* freedom, end of story. But isn't that only true if those choices are based on accurate perceptions? Therefore, our focus is best placed on making choices that result in getting better-quality data—in perceiving free of habits. Certain choices make it much easier to transcend context, culture, traumas, and habits and see the world and ourselves with less and less bias.

So, indeed, the choice is ours: Do we live as prisoners in a false world of habitual thoughts and emotions, living in separateness? Or can we come into the present moment and live in the light of interconnectedness and kindness?

CHAPTER 8

Relax
the
judging

An older man and his son went for a hike in the mountains. While they were hiking on a treacherous incline, they both fell. By the time the rescue crew arrived the older man was dead. They rushed his son to the hospital. An old physician examined the son and proclaimed, "He should be immediately rushed in for surgery, but I cannot operate on him. He is my son!"

Can you explain this paradox?

Okay. Here's another challenge:

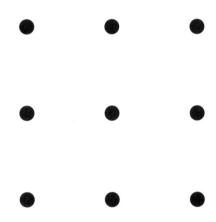

In the above figure, without taking your pencil off the page (or finger off your e-reader) cover all the dots by drawing no more than four straight lines. (Answers on page 138.)

Don't feel bad if you couldn't figure out these brain teasers. Most people get stumped by one or both of them. Even if they can figure out the answer, most people need a little bit of time to figure out why the answer isn't immediately obvious. That's because our habitual way of seeing things gets in the way. And it is those habits—especially as they relate to our interactions with others—that can lead us to jump to conclusions and trick us into not experiencing the world authentically.

> In the beginner's mind
> there are many possibilities,
> but in the expert's there are few.

—Shunryu Suzuki, *Zen Mind, Beginner's Mind*

Part of the way we solve problems is to make assumptions based on our past experience. These mental shortcuts do make a lot of problems easier to solve (especially problems that are similar to ones we encountered previously), but they can also lead us to make false assumptions and to bad decisions. A classic example with catastrophic results was the construction of the Maginot Line between France and Germany after World War I. The French generals assumed that any new war would be like the last one, but with better weapons, so they built an expensive fortified wall. However, the German generals invented a new kind of tactic, the blitzkrieg, and did the unimaginable and blew through weakly defended Holland and Belgium into an undefended part of France. Yikes!

We create our own mental Maginot Lines all the time without noticing. Scientists tell us that when we meet someone for the first time, we are already making important judgments about that person

Answer 1: The doctor is the son's mother.

Answer 2:

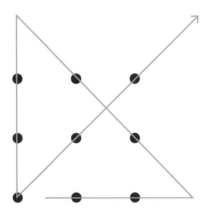

within a few milliseconds.[1] And within a few seconds after that, those judgments solidify and are very hard to change even when we are presented with new data. Maybe that's why sometimes we stick with that loser boyfriend when everyone around us already knows that it just ain't working out.

We have all experienced meeting someone and in a short time that person becomes someone whose name alone is enough to make our skin crawl. However, as time goes by something happens and we realize that person isn't horrible. We had totally misjudged him or her. We are unconscious judging machines (it all happens in those first few milliseconds), making false assumptions, and those judgments are often wrong or incomplete in possibly perilous, Maginot Line sorts of ways. As a result of a habitually conditioned reflex, a biological defense mechanism, or some combination of the two, these subtle and very quick judgments often cut us off from having warmhearted relations.

The good news is that you don't have to struggle against judging, which is a futile exercise. Instead you can just learn to relax your attitude about your judgments. Warmheartedness allows us to stay open and flexible and thus be able to receive new data or at least not take our judgments so seriously. By strengthening feelings of interconnectedness through the exercises we introduced in the last section, you are already quite a bit of the way there.

The next task is to work on specifically cultivating warmth—a wish for the other to be happy.

In part one you learned about *basic happiness*, about how to make the mind more flexible by practicing placing your attention in the present moment. It's a kind of cognitive training: instead of habitually reacting to thoughts and emotions, you remain fully present. In so doing, you gradually master your mind.

In part two you are learning about *interconnected happiness*, about how to work with your emotional life. Instead of closing yourself off to the reality of interconnectedness, you acknowledge it again and again. You return repeatedly to your natural capacity for warmth, kindness, and care. You transform your inner emotional life into openness and master your heart.

When you meet a best friend or that certain someone, that feeling of love transforms your entire world. Isn't it true that when you feel a special connection with one person it starts to influence all your relations? Suddenly you're more tolerant; you don't sweat the small stuff and sometimes even the big stuff.

By cultivating a strong sense of interdependence, we make it easier to feel warmheartedness. It is pretty obvious why: When we contemplate interdependence we become more aware of how much we depend on others and how much others depend on us. Not only do we begin to see ourselves in others. We see our fundamental commonality, the fact that we all want happiness and to minimize suffering. This insight of interconnectedness and commonality inspires a warming of the heart. Through warmheartedness, our actions gradually become defined by kindness and a generous spirit. As a result, our life becomes more and more meaningful. The satisfaction that arises *is* interconnected happiness: an open warming of the heart that carries us through sometimes turbulent emotions and habitual patterns of judgment. We gradually begin to master our heart and find meaningful contentment with our life.

So let's get into it.

This chapter introduces a set of meditations and exercises to help you cultivate warmheartedness. These practices have been used for over a thousand years in order to deepen insight and transform the practitioner's heart and mind. They are the outcome of much real-world beta testing.

If you take these practices into your life, you will begin to relax the judging, just as others have done. Although you will still judge, you will be more relaxed and open, and you will more easily change your mind when new data comes in. Experiencing interconnectedness through warm relations will be so much easier, and as the warmth shows you more interconnectedness, that will in turn inspire more warmth. The two go hand in hand.

CONSIDERING OTHERS AS IF THEY WERE ANOTHER YOU

• • • • • • • PHAKCHOK RINPOCHE • • • • • • •

As a child, I loved to visit with my grandfather Tulku Urgyen Rinpoche. Eventually, he would become my teacher, but when I was young he was just Grandfather. He had an uncanny ability to see what I needed and then adapt. If I was hungry, he would get me something delicious to eat. If I was bored, he would give me something to play with. When I was a little older, he would give me money when I needed to buy something important. I rarely had to say anything; he just had a knack for seeing things from my side and responding appropriately.

As I grew older and he became my teacher, I saw that this quality of his wasn't something that arose only due to our special connection. I would sometimes sit in his room as people from all over the Kathmandu Valley (and beyond) would make the several-hour hike up to his hermitage to visit him. He seemed to be able to tune in to the needs of whoever came to see him. Instead of giving what *he* wanted to give, he seemed to be able to see things from the other person's point of view, and he gave what *they* needed. It always started from their side, not from his side. For some it was money, others got medicine or food, for many it was an instruction on the most profound aspects of meditation. He seemed to possess an uncanny ability to see things from the other person's perspective—to empathize and understand what was required. No matter the need, my grandfather always seemed to find a way to meet it, in the warmest, most caring kind of way.

· · · · · · · · · · ·

What is the key to being able to understand and meet the needs of others? It is realizing that we are all pretty much the same. Just different permutations of human existence, each interacting with different circumstances. But still everyone wants to be happy and avoid suffering. The more you can identify with the basic commonality shared by all the myriad kinds of human existence, the easier it is to cultivate warm relations. In order to do this it helps to consider how in many ways other people are just another you.

CONSIDERING THE EQUALITY OF ALL

- Start by creating space and then do the Resting in the Light of Kindness exercise (page 133).

- Notice how each person in the web is a person who both received the kindness of others and also was kind to others. In this way we are all the same. No matter how fortunate we are, no matter how much trauma and pain we have had to endure, many other people in the unending lattice of support went through something just as good or just as bad. Everyone made it only because of the kindness of others, and each one passed on some kindness and care to someone else. In fact, everyone we know is here due to a similar lattice of support, which as you go back in time becomes larger and wider until it finally overlaps yours. We all have common roots of kindness and care.

- Imagine all the different lattices of support, stretching back in time, that each person alive today is part of. All are filled with people who—wanting to avoid suffering and desiring happiness—still found the time to be kind and caring to at least one other person. In this very fundamental way we are all pretty much the same.

- Imagine how everyone and his or her overlapping support web are bathed in the warm light of loving joy. No matter how much or how little support we have received, we are all still living proof of the kindness and care of others.

- Relax by dropping the contemplation for a few moments, and then focus on the breath or come back to creating space for a little while.

- Make the aspiration for everyone to be happy, to have the causes of happiness, and to be free from suffering and its causes.

EXCHANGING YOURSELF FOR OTHERS

- Think of someone you know who is suffering greatly. In the beginning, it's probably easier if it is someone you are fond of, but it could be someone you heard about in the news whose situation really moved you.

- Begin by creating space. Now imagine as much as possible how it would be if that suffering were yours. How would it feel to be going through that same misery? Consider how you would want people, including friends and family, to treat you. What would you most need from them?

- Make this exercise as vivid and real as possible. Really imagine how it feels. How would you want to be helped and in what particular ways by those around you?

- Then after a time, return to creating space or focusing on the breath.

- Make the aspiration for everyone to be happy, to have the causes of happiness, and to be free from suffering and its causes.

When you consider the equality of all and mentally exchange yourself for others again and again, it becomes easier and easier to consider others as if they were another you.

SHARING HAPPINESS

Now that you have considered how others are like another you, we are going to explain how to imagine sharing happiness with and relieving the suffering of people you are close to. Before you start the practice, think of a few people closest to you whom you want to share with— best friends, lovers, or close relatives. Gradually you will widen the scope of the sharing to include everybody.

EXPERIENCING AND SHARING JOY

- Begin by creating space.

- After a few minutes, recall a time when you were a child (or later if need be) when you felt truly carefree and happy. Remember everything about this time: where you were, the room you were in, or, if it was outside, the details of the setting. Recall any distinctive sights, sounds, or smells. But most of all remember how it felt to be so carefree and full of joy. Really get into it; make it as vivid as possible. (If you have trouble recalling a carefree time, do the Resting in the Light of Kindness exercise.)

- Feel your heart open. Then consider that any tension in your body subsides and you allow yourself to fully reexperience this carefree joy from years ago.

- Imagine the joy is also manifesting as a soft light that surrounds you. Rest in the sensation of the soft light of delight for a time.

- Now imagine that the person you feel closest to is right in front of you. Share this feeling of carefree happiness with her. Invite her to share this feeling of joy that you experienced before and are reexperiencing again. Allow the soft light of happiness to wash over her, completely. As the delightful feeling of carefree joy opens her heart, all the tension and pain in her body is dissolved and she relaxes. Her face breaks into a sweet, simple smile as she enjoys this carefree feeling. Rest together with her in this vivid state of joy, bathed in soft light, for a little while.

- Next, imagine a few people who are extremely close to you appearing in front of you. As before, share this feeling of happiness and well-being that you experienced before and are experiencing again right now. Watch as the soft light of happiness enters their body, and all the tension and pain are released. As they relax, a gentle grin alights on each of their faces. Rest together with your closest loved ones, all enjoying this joyful feeling. Imagine a gentle orb of light envelops you all.

- You can expand this field of joy even further. Imagine inviting a group of people you really like. Maybe they are colleagues at work or from your social network. Share the light of happiness as before. Invite them to experience the same joy you are experiencing. Let it dissolve all the tension and pain. And then rest with them.

- If you are new to this practice, this might be a good place to stop—first, by returning to creating space or by putting your focus on the breath.

- End with the aspiration for everyone to be happy, to have the causes of happiness, and to be free from suffering and its causes.

SHARING JOY: STRANGERS AND ENEMIES

After becoming more familiar with the practice in the Experiencing and Sharing Joy exercise, you can expand the field of joy even further to people you don't know.

- Start the same way as the previous exercise, except now recall a person you saw on the street or the person you get a coffee from in the morning, or anyone you don't know well, at all, or else feel neutral about. Invite as many neutral people as you can think of into the orb of light. Their bodies relax as any tension or pain is released, and they smile.

- After doing that for a time, try including people who annoy you. Invite them into your field of joy. Allow the gentle orb of light to wash over them and relieve them of their tension and pain. Watch as they relax and grin with delight. Laugh with them. Welcome them and share the incredible gift of carefree happiness. In this state, there is no annoyance, no judging, no problems of any kind—just the soft, gentle light of delight filled with all your friends and acquaintances and maybe even a few people who generally annoy you.

- After you become used to sharing with people who annoy you, try inviting into the circle people who have done you real harm, your enemies. Or it could be really bad people you learn about on the news. But no matter how bad they are, invite them in. Share as you did before. Allow the light of delight to heal them and grin together with all of them. Then rest in the soft light of carefree joy.

- Return to creating space or focusing on the breath. End with the aspiration for everyone to be happy, to have the causes of happiness, and to be free from suffering and its causes.

Sharing joy with enemies can be very challenging, and it takes practice. Don't worry about doing it perfectly or beating yourself up if a bunch of turbulent emotions arise. Be gentle and patient with yourself. Eventually, you will be able to invite the entire world into your field of joy. And as you do so, you will relax the judging even more.

LEARNING TO RELAX THE JUDGING

As mentioned earlier, scientific studies have come out in the last ten years that show we form strong opinions about people in milliseconds. These opinions are very difficult to change and sometimes wrong. We have all had the experience of not liking someone until we got to know them better. Yet we make lots of decisions based on this primal, habitual brain function. This kind of process of judgment is coloring our view, preventing us from experiencing the world authentically. But the good news is that we can learn to relax this habit of making quick judgments through cultivating loving-kindness and compassion during meditation, as well as learning to celebrate the good fortune of others.

· · · · · · · · · ERRIC SOLOMON · · · · · · · · ·

I was asked to give meditation classes in a minimum-security prison in California. One of the guys in class who was most enthusiastic about the subject was also quite a character. For this story I'll call him Bill.

Bill was a fisherman who found he could make a lot more money smuggling weed from Thailand than by fishing. When he started out, he was a peace-and-love guy, but as the smuggling became more and more successful he started becoming quite paranoid and reckless, and he also started carrying guns. Now, though, he felt that prison likely saved him from a much worse fate. Nevertheless, as you might imagine, a few pesky thoughts still gnawed at Bill.

When we did the Experiencing and Sharing Joy practice together with the group of inmates who were attending the class, Bill was all-in. That is, until we got to the sharing with enemies part. He really lost it. He got over-the-top upset, and we had to stop the practice. It turns out that while Bill was taking a six-year timeout, his former partner, who ratted on him, was sitting on the French Riviera with several million of Bill's bills. "How can I invite him into my field of joy?" shouted Bill.

Many of those in the class were sharing cells, and they hung out a lot together and knew each other's stories quite well. One of them asked Bill if he was happy when he had all that money. Bill shot back, "You know I wasn't. I was walking around with a gun, worried all the time that someone was out to get me."

Another inmate dared to suggest that Bill's partner took the money in order to be happy. He went on to point out that when Bill had the money it didn't make him happy. The other guys piled on, teasing and laughing at Bill, "He took the money to be happy, yet he was looking in the wrong place for happiness." Bill tried gamely to suggest that it's better to have the money than not, but you could already see he was losing steam. Another guy yelled, "Just remember how bad you felt when you had all that money. Why are you still dwelling on that stuff, man?" It might be hard to understand how the brutality of prison humor helps anyone shake something like that off, but on that day I witnessed it.

It wasn't that Bill just dropped it then and there completely. But he did start laughing a bit with all the teasing going on. He later said it was the first time in six years he could begin to start letting go of his anger and hurt. He kept trying to share joy with his former business partner who ratted him out. And he eventually found a way out of the psychological prison he had put himself in.

. . . .

MAKING ASPIRATIONS FOR EVERYONE TO BE HAPPY

As you likely noticed, at the end of each exercise in this chapter we suggest you make an aspiration for everyone to be happy, to have the causes of happiness, and to be free from suffering and its causes. It's a wish we make in order to end the practice with the same positive motivation we started with. Since our actions are the result of our thoughts, it is good to end our session with the aspiration that others may experience happiness and be free from sorrow.

The word *aspiration* has two meanings: the desire to attain a goal as well as the act of breathing. So bring these two meanings together and create thoughts on the breath that will influence your actions after you end your practice session.

At the end of our practice session, as you exhale, imagine that the universe is touched by the warm light of happiness that radiates from your warmhearted feeling. All beings, all inanimate objects, are bathed in the warm light. As you breathe in, think, "I wish that all beings are free from sorrow and its causes." Into the spaciousness, the vast expanse of the universe, the light of our warmheartedness permeates everyone and everything.

Do this for as long as you can, but at a minimum, do three inhalations and three exhalations. Breathe in the desire for everyone to be free from suffering. Breathe out the warm gentle light of happiness, wishing that everyone is touched by it and is happy.

People sometimes criticize the practice of sending aspirations as merely a way to feel good without actually *doing* anything to help people. But everything, every action, starts with a single moment of thought. A single thought of kindness, of wishing for others to be happy, will lead to actions that provide succor. These actions are the result of our aspirations—a single moment of thought. That single thought has the potential to create a tsunami of results.

CHAPTER 9

Be Attentive

Kindness goes a long ways lots of times
when it ought to stay at home.

—Kin Hubbard

We find interconnected happiness by resolving a paradox. Although we experience the full measure of interconnected happiness through interacting with others, those very interactions can be our biggest obstacles. When our interactions spark understanding, kindness, or caring, interconnected happiness is ours to enjoy. But when they result in anger, closed-mindedness, or a cold heart, interconnected happiness can become an abstract idea at best.

The key to this chapter is the practice of transforming daily interactions with other people into a powerful support for warmheartedness. This means we get more life satisfaction and contentment—the fruit of interconnected happiness. A cool side effect is that it benefits nearly everybody we interact with too. By learning to be attentive, you will be able to integrate the insight, empathy, and caring you experienced during the exercises in the last two chapters into daily activities.

Attentiveness means that we pay attention to others and react to them in a caring way. The approach we discussed earlier of treating difficult thoughts and emotions in the same way an experienced host would treat invited guests can apply to interacting with other people too. An experienced host attends to the needs of a difficult guest with kindness and care, to keep the party fun for everyone. In the same way, by approaching others in harmony with the interconnected nature of reality, our attitude is one of attentiveness—kindness and care. Then everyone benefits, especially the one being attentive.

THE FOUR JOYFUL SUPPORTS

Practicing the exercises in chapters 4 and 5 will be a big help. But now we go beyond that to explore how to integrate that feeling of interconnectedness and warmth into interactions with people, especially the difficult ones. The way to keep ourselves from an unnecessary preoccupation with self-protective behavior—the enemy of experiencing the happiness of interconnectedness—is through the four joyful supports:

GENEROSITY

PATIENCE

CONSISTENCY

COMMITMENT

These help us care for others and nurture ourselves at the same time. They also bring more humor and joy into our lives and, perhaps more importantly, bring us greater satisfaction and support the sense of our lives having meaning.

It takes generosity to discover the whole through others. If you realize you are only a violin, you can open yourself up to the world by playing your role in the concert.

—Jacques Yves Cousteau

GENEROSITY

After practicing the exercises in this book again and again, kindness begins to come automatically when you simply feel what it is like to be the other person.

· · · · · · · PHAKCHOK RINPOCHE · · · · · · ·

The other day I was coming out of a coffee shop and saw a homeless man lying on some cardboard. It was quite cold out, and the man was obviously not well. He had some sort of disfiguring growth on his face that he was trying to hide by turning his head.

I imagined what it would be like to be him, sleeping on cardboard, outside in the cold, with no one daring to look at me or care for me at all. I turned around and went back into the shop. I ordered a hot sandwich and some coffee, put some money in a napkin, and brought it out to the man. I knelt down and handed it to him. I sat next to him and we talked.

He was so grateful for the food but also for the company and for the respect. I tried my best not to look down on him but showed interest in whatever he had to say. I can still see the way his eyes went from dull to bright, and the warm smile that slowly crossed his face.

. . . .

Generosity is freely giving good things to others as abundantly as possible in order to enhance others' well-being. Generosity isn't limited to money and possessions; it can also refer to offerings such as time, attention, aid, encouragement, emotional availability, and respect. It's a natural expression of living in harmony with the interconnected nature of reality—*your* well-being is intimately tied to my own.

All of us can be quite stingy, spending more time and effort trying to hold on to what we have than to giving. You may think you're actually quite generous, and it's probably true that in many ways you are. But every time you try to hold on to something, even an experience or an idea, that's a subtle form of stinginess. We've already spent a lot of time looking at how we try to hold on to or extend the good stuff, but we have also seen how this kind of clinging actually causes a lot of problems. Acting with a spirit of generosity not only helps the person who is the object of your benevolence but it helps you as well. It's interconnected!

Try imagining a world without any generosity—everyone just worrying about his or her own needs and ignoring everybody else's. How could that be anything but wretched, radical unhappiness?

When you give, it's important to do so without hoping to get something in return. True generosity should not be like a business investment. Give happily and wholeheartedly, whatever the situation—be it family, business, or volunteering to help out at a charity. This is really important.

For example, if a friend is going through a difficult time—perhaps she has lost her job, is having family and financial troubles, or is simply feeling downhearted—then give up some of your time to go and see her and talk to her. Lend her your support. If you see a beggar, consider giving material support like food, blankets, or money, but also give him a smile when you do it. If you encounter a very stubborn, bossy person—maybe it's even your supervisor at work—give her your respect, since that's most likely what she wants and needs.

When someone behaves in a way we don't like or agree with, we usually start to resist, to tighten up, and then act out of our resistance. But, with an attitude of generosity, like an experienced party host, you can think, "how can I give this person what they want?" Maybe just listening wholeheartedly will do the trick. Or showing you understand. Even if it is in the office and you are having a disagreement about how to go about something vital to the business, you can still give the other person your time, respect, and understanding.

> If you haven't any charity in your heart,
> you have the worst kind of heart trouble.
>
> —Bob Hope

EXERCISE 22

PRACTICING GENEROSITY

This practice expands on the Experiencing and Sharing Joy exercise (page 146). Sharing joy is a kind of generosity, don't you think?

- Practice the Experiencing and Sharing Joy exercise.

- Just before you end the session, make the aspiration to approach the world with an attitude of generosity. Consider the day ahead: Can you imagine anything that might arise that could be an opportunity to be generous? Is there an interaction coming up that usually triggers a counterproductive habitual reaction? Imagine instead reacting generously.

- Return to creating space or focusing on the breath for a few minutes.

- End the session by considering your heartfelt aspiration for everyone to be happy, to have the causes of happiness, and to be free from suffering and its causes.

If you learn to enjoy waiting,
you don't have to wait to enjoy.

—Kazuaki Tanahashi

The key to everything is patience.
You get the chicken by hatching the egg,
not by smashing it.

—Arnold H. Glasow

PATIENCE

If you are a generous person but short-tempered, you won't get to enjoy interconnected happiness—people will hesitate to hang out with you because it could be really unpleasant. The solution is to be patient, not irritable. But patience does not mean keeping your anger locked up inside behind a smiling face. That might be good for the people around you, but it will create big problems for you. If you keep hatred, rage, or ill will in your heart, it will slowly grow, like a small flame that grows into a blazing fire, until it ends up consuming you completely. So for your own sake, be patient from the bottom of your heart. And once again, like generosity, patience has the cool side effect of being beneficial for others too.

To learn to be more patient you first need to convince yourself that anger won't solve any problems; in fact, it will likely make things worse. It is just a habitual response to what is usually unreliable data. We have all had the experience of looking back sheepishly on a time when we were angry and realize now that we were jumping to conclusions. Being angry will not undo any harm or mistakes that have been made. Being angry will not make you or others happy, nor will it bring you respect or power. So what's the use of getting angry? Be patient. Then you will be clearheaded and able to make the best possible decision, and you and those around you will also suffer a lot less.

When you do manage to be patient, try not to engage in thoughts such as, "I am being so patient toward this colleague. She is really so trying to be around, but I am being extremely patient. I am really doing her a favor," because this kind of attitude could end up backfiring on you later on. When you are patient in this self-centered way, you are not living in harmony with interdependence. You are just subtly reifying your self-referential point of view. Real patience is always coming from true generosity, a gift you give without any notion of getting something in return.

In practicing generosity, the emphasis is on honoring the interconnected nature of reality. While learning to become patient, your emphasis should be on being spacious. When you are spacious, you won't respond habitually out of anger. Spaciousness is the basis for patience, and in that space you have the freedom to choose your actions. This is why, if you want to be more patient, taking a couple of creating space mini-breaks during the day will help support your intentions.

How poor are they that have not patience!
What wound did ever heal but by degrees?
—William Shakespeare

PRACTICING PATIENCE

This is almost exactly like what you do when you want to work on your generosity.

- Start your day with the Experiencing and Sharing Joy exercise (page 146).

- Consider the day ahead: Can you imagine anything that might arise that could be an opportunity to be patient? Or is there an interaction coming up today that usually triggers your anger or enmity? Imagine instead not immediately reacting but rather responding by giving space. That is the key to patience.

- At the end of the exercise, return to creating space or focusing on the breath for a few minutes and make the aspiration to approach the world with patience.

- End the session by considering your heartfelt aspiration for everyone to be happy and to be free from suffering and its causes.

- Now begin the rest of your day.

Between stimulus and response there is a space.
In that space is our power to choose our response.
In our response lies our growth and our freedom.
—Viktor Frankl

CONSISTENCY

We mentioned consistency in our discussion of basic happiness back in chapter 6 (page 103), but now let's see how that applies to interconnected happiness.

Generosity and patience are excellent qualities, but they need support. If we are lazy, we will never accomplish anything. If we want to play an instrument, become an awesomely great hacker, an innovative artist, a doctor, a lawyer, or be way more kind and caring, we need to apply ourselves—not just now and then when we're in the right mood but regularly no matter what. So we apply our efforts with enthusiastic consistency, which means—with a positive motivation—doing something we enjoy that benefits ourselves and others. You can start gradually, such as with your family or friends. This is so important, because when you do something you enjoy and see that it also benefits your family and others, this will bring you real interconnected joy, a kind of inner joy that cannot be bought.

Some folks say that most people do good deeds only because of the happiness and satisfaction it brings them, so actually they are just as selfish as anyone else. But let's examine this carefully. For example, imagine two people who each have $100,000. The first one decides to do something for others with her money, with a true motive to be of service, a sincere wish to help, but also knowing that she's going to feel happy about having done it. The second person doesn't give a single dollar away to others but keeps it all for himself. Yes, he lives very comfortably, but because of his selfish attitude he does not get any real, inner joy out of this. Is there really no difference between these two individuals?

Ultimately, giving with a mind-set of also wishing to gain some happiness or good feelings for yourself is not genuine generosity, because you are lost in the realm of grasping after your hopes and worrying about your fears. The result of grasping is not positive at all, as we have seen. So if you have embarked on cultivating generosity and patience, it is best if you can free yourself from getting too caught up in results.

Of course, it's very difficult to be totally free of any wish to get at least a little benefit from the practice. It's natural to expect something. In fact, at the beginning we need some kind of motivation to start. No one is reading this book because he or she is mostly interested in the happiness of others. The key thing is to recognize the flaw and notice when you become too preoccupied with results. Have a sense of humor about the paradoxical nature of the endeavor and develop an enthusiasm for playing with and against your mind's habitual tendencies. Generally speaking, giving, or doing any other positive act with a sincere wish to benefit others naturally makes you feel happy, but do not get attached to this feeling and do good acts only for that feeling alone.

In this spirit, in order to gain stability in living in accord with the fundamental nature of reality, make generosity and patience the focus of your daily interactions. This regular expression of kindness and care is how to be consistent.

As we discussed in chapter 6, "Be Present," as you bring new practices into your life it's important to commit to an achievable number of minutes of meditation a day. As you shift from the basic happiness practices to the interconnected happiness exercises, remind yourself to be consistent in your practice.

Start with a reasonable minimum goal, something you know you can do, and build from there. Promise yourself you will do a few minutes a day for three days. At the end of three days, consider increasing the number of minutes you practice by another minute or three. Commit to doing this for three or four days. Slowly build up the number of minutes of practice and the number of days you commit to.

WARMHEARTED MINI-BREAK

You can also integrate warmheartedness into your day by taking warmhearted mini-breaks.

- Whenever you have a few spare minutes, sit quietly and *make the aspiration for everyone to be happy*.

- As you breathe in, think *may all beings be free from sorrow and suffering*.

- As you breathe out, send the warm light of happiness from your heart out into the farthest reaches of space.

- Consider that it touches everyone, and they become content and worry-free.

- As you breathe out, think *may everyone be happy*.

Try practicing this for at least three breaths, but of course if you have time, do more!

COMMITMENT

How can we become even more consistent in our actions so that the view of interconnectedness permeates nearly everything we do? It is important to make a commitment to the process of learning to live in harmony with interconnectedness. We need to be honest with ourselves about where we need to improve. If you never notice your own problems and don't make any effort to improve—whether those problems are emotional, physical, in your relationships, or at work— you will continue to encounter them time and time again, and things will just get worse. So we need to get to know ourselves well. We need to look at our faults and accept them. This is such an important quality. Traditionally, we call this *discipline*.

Most people think discipline means rules like "Do this. Don't do that," but the real discipline comes by making a commitment to noticing and accepting your own faults and mistakes.

Try this out: Raise your index finger, point it at your face, and imagine that someone you find unbelievably annoying is pointing at you, saying, "You're a stingy, angry, short-tempered loser. You're a liar!" Then watch your mind. Instead of succumbing to anger or defensiveness, try asking yourself, is it true? Am I really stingy? Am I really angry and short-tempered? Be honest with yourself, no one has to know the answer except you.

I had been a manager for about eighteen months, when my boss called me into his office for my performance review. My previous manager had left the company about six months before to join a start-up. I liked Jim, my new supervisor, a lot. He was fair, he set clear, achievable goals, and he had a lot of experience I could learn from. So I was pretty stunned when I got my review.

Jim did mention my accomplishments, but I somehow couldn't hear any of that. All I heard was the mountain of things I didn't do well. I was often irritated by small things, didn't keep my emotions in proper check, was too quick to dress down colleagues and reports. The list went on and on. Devastated, I went home and began to dust off my résumé.

At first, I was lost in turbulent thoughts about how Jim hadn't been my manager long enough to say those things. Mentally, I defended myself against all these accusations. I became more and more self-righteous. After I finished updating my résumé, I knew I needed to change the mental conversation I was having. I went out for a long walk in the mountains above Silicon Valley. As I exhausted myself on the long climb, and took in the spacious beauty of the Santa Cruz Mountains under the spectacular blue California sky, my mind calmed down. I found a good spot on the trail with a fabulous vista overlooking the valley and sat down to take it all in.

Gradually, I started to reflect on my situation. I began to see that Jim had actually made a few good points about my behavior. After all, like most young high-tech managers, I had been promoted for my technical acumen rather than my people skills. So I shouldn't have been surprised that I still had a lot to learn. Furthermore, I saw how many of the things Jim said to me other people had probably noticed too. Jim was just the only one who cared enough to say the truth. In fact, he probably was bothering to tell me because he believed in my potential.

The more I looked at my situation, without lots of judgment about how bad I was or wasn't, the more I saw that most of the stuff, if not all, that Jim

was describing were things I ought to want to work on in myself, whether I was at this job, at home, or any place else. I decided to give Jim at least another six months and never sent out that nicely polished résumé.

. . . .

Even when someone gently points out our faults, we usually become a little bit defensive. And who is harmed by that? We are, because we are missing out on the opportunity to improve ourselves. We will continue to create the same difficulties for ourselves and others. So don't wait for other people to point their fingers at you, but point your own finger at yourself and check whether or not you are living in harmony with interconnectedness. Are you as kind, generous, and patient as you could be or is there an opportunity for growth?

Another aspect of commitment is right behavior or ethics. If you act in a very strange, rude, or outrageous way, people might get offended or annoyed and try to avoid you. This probably won't make you that happy either. Of course you might think, "I don't care what others think or what they say. I'm going to do whatever I like." You may tell yourself that doing what *you* want without caring what others think *is* freedom and therefore meaningful. However, there are others who are more careful about what they do and pay attention to what others say and think; for them, that is a meaningful way of life. Ultimately, of course, it's up to you which path you choose, but let's examine the options.

If you live according to the first idea—doing whatever you like— there will never be an end to it, because you are just slavishly chasing after your desires and wishes without a second thought. And we hope we have convinced you by now that your desires, things you like and want to possess or keep, are endless. Indulging in them will never lead to contentment but rather keep you locked in a prison of continuous dissatisfaction. So it's important to think about how you behave, how you talk, and how you interact with others. Ethics here means behaving and speaking in an appropriate manner—being generous and patient. It means speaking kindly, being polite, considerate, respectful, and so on. But this should not be superficial or two-faced. What you think, say, and actually do should be similar. Sometimes it is difficult to make what you think, say, and do exactly the same, especially in the beginning, but try to make them at least similar. Honestly ask yourself if you think you will be able to lead a peaceful, meaningful life without this simple kind of ethics.

Another way to think about ethics is to ask yourself which kind of behavior is more likely to cause you to experience yourself, others, and the world around you in a more authentic, accurate manner. Is it by living in harmony with interconnectedness, or by a narcissistic focus on your own needs? If you examine each action you're thinking of taking in this light, you don't need lots of ethical rules to follow. You can evaluate your actions based on a desire to experience everything free of habitually biased judgments and conditioned responses. When you view things from this perspective, a lot of the time it's pretty easy to know what to do.

So, we need these three kinds of commitment: noticing our own faults but without judging ourselves; being willing to work on improving ourselves; and maintaining basic ethics.

Weakness of attitude becomes weakness of character.

—Albert Einstein

PRACTICING COMMITMENT

The point of this exercise is to get used to identifying and accepting your foibles, faults, or opportunities to get better in tune with interconnected happiness. You can also use this exercise to look at obstacles in your life, vexing problems, or people who are causing stress.

- Start by creating space.

- After you have settled into the practice, look at the last twenty-four hours. Ask yourself the following kinds of questions:

  – Have I been as kind, generous, and patient as possible?

  – Was I honest in my dealings with others?

  – Did I consider others' needs?

  – Did I indulge too much in self-centered concerns?

- Don't forget about relaxing the comparing; there is no need to judge yourself or compare yourself to others. Within space there is plenty of room for our flaws; they do not define us. You can change, grow, and overcome anything with a bit of generosity and patience. Just be as open and honest with yourself as possible. Be kind to yourself, the way you would if it were a close family member or friend who was looking to overcome their flaws. Just allow yourself the chance to observe any of life's challenges while resting in spaciousness.

- Is there something you can commit to doing that will improve the situation, even if it is only a little bit? Make a promise to yourself to work on yourself; imagine yourself overcoming this obstacle.

- End the session by making a heartfelt aspiration for everyone to be happy, to have the causes of happiness, and to be free from suffering and its causes.

A DAILY PLAN FOR INTERCONNECTED HAPPINESS

Let's bring together all the different interconnected happiness exercises from part two into a plan for your day. We suggest focusing on one practice at a time before moving on to the next. Ideally, over the course of four months, you should practice each exercise for two weeks before moving on to the next, and spend one month on Experiencing and Sharing Joy. This will help you to exercise your interconnected happiness muscle in a thoughtful way.

······ INTERCONNECTED ······ HAPPINESS

MORNING

Awake with happiness. In your first moments of conscious awareness, imagine how you will be kind and caring, generous and patient during the day. Make an aspiration that today your actions will help others be happy or help relieve their discontent or suffering.

·

Interconnected happiness exercise (10–15 minutes). Pick one of the exercises explained in this part and do it. Imagine how you will take a few warmhearted mini-breaks during the day and what your trigger will be. Make an aspiration for everyone to be happy. Now start your day.

AFTERNOON

Warmhearted mini-breaks. In small pockets throughout the day—while waiting for a movie to begin, riding on the bus, instead of checking Facebook—practice creating space and focusing on your breath, and practice generosity. Count your mini-breaks and gradually increase the number of mini-breaks you take each day.

EVENING

Commitment and consistency practices (10 minutes). Reflect on how, despite a lifetime spent mostly chasing self-absorbed distraction, you spent a bit of time practicing caring for others.

·

Celebrate. Celebrate the few moments you were kind, patient, and generous or at least didn't succumb to habitual negative ways of reacting. Then visualize yourself doing it again tomorrow. Make aspirations for the happiness of everyone!

PART THREE

RADICAL
HAPPINESS

Mastering Dignity

Remember Phakchok Rinpoche's story about the difference between throwing stones at a dog and a lion at the beginning of the book? When you throw stones at a dog, he chases after the stones. A lion, on the other hand, doesn't worry about the stones at all. Instead, he looks to see where the stones are coming from. When we turn our attention toward the present moment, instead of chasing each thought, we take the first step toward being more like a lion than a dog.

But this is just the first step. Next, just like a lion, you can begin to look at the stone thrower. You can learn to look at the source of the thoughts themselves. And that's the secret to being radically happy.

Is it really that easy? Yes—and no. For most of us, there are a few helpful steps to take to make sure we really understand how to do it.

So, let's begin by taking a good look at our lion friend. A lion knows it is powerful; she has confidence in her power. It isn't a braggy, egotistical confidence; a lion just knows her own strength. So, when a stone comes, she doesn't waste time; she just turns her gaze. Usually, that is enough. Imagine you are throwing stones at a lion. When her head turns to look, don't you think you will run? And if you don't, the lion eats you. Either way, you are gone—and so are the stones!

Mastering dignity is the heart of radical happiness. It begins with cultivating a quiet self-confidence in the power of the exercises, contemplations, and meditations you have learned—both the exercises you've learned in this book and any others you may learn that complement those methods. Through these practices you develop a conviction that these meditative methods are a way to establish basic and interconnected happiness in your life, and having done so, radical happiness will emerge.

This conviction in our own path to radical happiness is very different from egocentric pride or confidence. Egocentric pride and confidence are always just a way to cover up or hide from your own lack of self-esteem. Normal pride or confidence is based on comparison. People are usually proud of their talents because of how those talents stack up against others' talents. We normally have confidence and take pride in one of the qualities we have that we consider to be better than normal. It marks us as above average. But this self-centered way of relating to ourselves is very fragile, because when someone is better than us in a given way or on any given day we can easily become jealous or angry. When we know about our qualities and value them *in and of themselves,* no matter how small or large they may be, we have dignity. When we have confidence in our own qualities, we are not threatened by someone being better, faster, or smarter: another's talents don't diminish our own. We don't fall into the trap of low self-esteem or apathy. Instead, we still have confidence in our own talents and may even take pleasure in other people's abilities as well.

In this chapter we will give you a couple of new practices that are subtle, yet radically transformative. Most of us spend an entire lifetime chasing thoughts and emotions like a dog, never finding complete satisfaction. Yet, with a *slight but radical* shift of attention, we turn toward the stone thrower—awareness itself. Radical happiness is about developing dignity, becoming like a lion—understanding our natural awareness, gaining confidence in it, and turning toward awareness instead of toward habitually rising thoughts and emotions. It's a little bit subtle and may take some time, but once you get the hang of it, it is a treasure no one can steal away. And that treasure is the result of a radical transformation in how we view ourselves and our world.

THE THREE KEYS TO RADICAL HAPPINESS

1. Cultivating dignity.

By bringing basic and interconnected happiness into a unified whole we deepen our confidence in these practices. In order to develop a firm foundation for experiencing radical happiness we need a quiet confidence in basic and interconnected happiness. That confidence comes from understanding the reasoning behind how the practices function, and experiencing the results of the exercises. Just like when you practice a musical instrument and your playing improves, you gain confidence in your ability to play.

2. Relax the clinging.

We use thoughts and emotions to relax and release our subtle habitual tendencies. By looking directly at them, these tendencies dissolve, and we rest in objectless meditation.

3. Be aware.

We turn our attention directly toward the stone thrower—the knowing quality of mind—the final key to being radically happy. At the moment of looking into the knowing quality of mind, we are free of all the stones of habitual thinking and can rest our attention in pure awareness.

CHAPTER 10

Cultivating Dignity

· · · · · · · · ERRIC SOLOMON · · · · · · · ·

In the beginning of *Radically Happy*, I told a story about my personal financial meltdown, followed by my narcissistic wallow and a phone call from one of my main teachers. To refresh your memory, he told me, "Right now everything is fine. Don't think too much about yourself." Over time I have come to understand this simple statement in a few important ways. First, Rinpoche was reminding me of the essence of basic happiness ("Right now everything is fine") as well as the essence of interconnected happiness ("Don't think about yourself too much," which meant think about others' needs). And then he hung up the phone.

Why? Because he had confidence in me. Or perhaps more accurately, he had confidence that if I applied what I had learned from practicing, I would be fine. All he had to do was give me an abrupt poke. It is true that he didn't spell it all out, but that's how it works sometimes when the teacher is really skilled. Rinpoche just interrupted my habitual pattern enough that I could connect the dots. But really as wonderful and empowering as his confidence in me was, it wouldn't have been helpful if I didn't also have confidence in the methods for coming into the present moment, and for not becoming too self-absorbed by my own problems so that I could think of other people too.

· · · · · · · · · · · ·

Just like a lion has the quiet dignity that results from knowing his own ability, you will gradually gain confidence that the methods of basic and interconnected happiness can radically transform your mind. When you have simple confidence in the power of the exercises, contemplations, and meditations described in the book, then the magic of being radically happy will arise as a by-product. Dignity is that simple confidence that comes from experiencing the effectiveness of the methods we've shared here.

You can begin by bringing basic and interconnected happiness together into a unified whole. When you are in the present-moment experience of basic happiness, you no longer are distracted by involuntarily chasing your thoughts. Through cultivating a consistent attention to the needs of others—the basis of interconnected happiness—you appreciate and begin to live in accord with the natural interdependence between yourself and the world and all its inhabitants. These methods enhance and support each other.

We need the strength of meditation's mindful awareness to stabilize love and compassion so that it begins to rise in every situation. When we think of others, we forget about ourselves. The preoccupation with ourselves is the very basis for the constant measuring of experience, comparing ourselves with others, and thinking of how we'd like things to be. At the moment when great love and caring for others become predominant in our mind, our habitually self-centered way of thinking has completely dissolved. At that moment, if we have been training ourselves in being present, we can experience ourselves and the world around us in a radically different way—unaffected by our usual habitual patterns of thoughts and emotions. That way of being is the essence of being radically happy.

THE WAY TO CULTIVATE DIGNITY AND CONFIDENCE

So, how do you cultivate the dignity that results from basic and interconnected happiness? This dignity and confidence comes through understanding, exercising, and experiencing. In this user's guide for the mind, we have used understanding and exercising so that our mind has an experience—a taste of basic, interconnected, and radical happiness.

Understanding comes from thinking about the logical reasons for basic and interconnected happiness explained in the previous chapters. It is helpful to go through those explanations, wrestle with them, argue them out in your mind or with others, until you are confident in the reasoning. It is through understanding that you will begin to have confidence that there is a specific result from practicing basic happiness (present-moment awareness) and a specific result from practicing interconnected happiness (warmheartedness).

Exercising means that we practice the contemplations and meditations again and again. Just like going to the gym helps our body to stay fit, repeatedly working with our mind in an enthusiastic, consistent manner results in mental and emotional well-being.

Experience is the result of understanding and exercising. When you have good understanding and you exercise your mind again and again, you will gain experience. And experience leads to a quiet dignity that enhances your confidence in the methods, which means you will employ them more often and more effectively.

The foundation for dignity is having confidence in the realization that the seed of happiness is already present within your mind. As your experience of basic and interconnected happiness becomes more and more familiar, you will begin to see that the seed for happiness was always there within your mind. You will see:

Present-moment awareness
was always available.

•

Warmheartedness is your natural condition
when all the neurotic habits are dissolved.

•

You already possess within your mind all the
ingredients for happiness and well-being.

•

It is through understanding and exercise
that you gain this experience.

•

It is through this experience that you gain
an unshakable, self-assured dignity.

The more you can bring basic and interconnected happiness together, the easier it will be for dignity to arise. You will become like a lion who knows his own strength. He doesn't need to dwell on it or compare his talents to anyone else's. He isn't insecure, constantly thinking, "I am so powerful, I am so ferocious, look at how they all fear me!" He doesn't need to waste time on building himself up. He just knows what he knows; he has the confidence that comes from dignity.

As you bring basic and interconnected happiness together, you will be able to transcend subtle clinging to outcomes and experiences. These subtle kinds of attachment can result from practicing either basic or interconnected happiness on its own.

For example, as you become basically happy, there may come a slight fondness for or expectation of experiencing the peace that is discovered in meditation practice. This subtle clinging to peace might lead you to reject the normal chaos and discomfort that comes along with being out in the world interacting with others. If that happens, you are once again in the land of depending on circumstances.

However, as you gain familiarity with being interconnectedly happy, it is easy to develop a slight attachment to *the agenda* of helping others and how it makes you feel, or to be subtly holding on to the expectation that you will be recognized for your good deeds. At that point you can get caught up in measuring, comparing, and judging.

THE WINGS OF THE BIRD

Earlier in this book we talked about basic happiness practice and interconnected happiness practice as separate things. And in the beginning, that is the best way to practice. But now, in order to practice radical happiness, it is necessary to practice the two together. A bird needs two wings to fly: both wings are part of the same bird. Just so, we need both present-moment awareness and present-moment warmheartedness in order to soar into radical happiness.

By practicing basic happiness and interconnected happiness together at the same time, we can overcome even a subtle fondness for the peace of meditation. This is because we learn to be fully present while being attentive to our interactions with other people. We get used to being present without requiring the world to be peaceful and calm. Remaining present while acting for the welfare of ourselves and everyone else, we are able to be free of too much attachment to the outcome or being recognized for our deeds. This is because being present cuts through the habitual evaluation of our actions.

It's not that these subtle kinds of clinging are so bad. In fact it's a great sign of progress to have these concerns. Yet, being radically happy is the result of the dignity that comes from knowing how to live free from the grip of constant expectations and doubts. Free of self-centeredness, we gain confident dignity when we know that the seed of contentment and well-being is always with us in any activity. This kind of radically happy dignity is the source of respect, care, and love for ourselves and everybody else.

CHAPTER 11

Relax
the,
Clinging

P erhaps you have heard the Yiddish term *kvetch*. Generally speaking, it refers to a sort of incessant whining and complaining, usually about relatively trivial things. It was a very common habit in my family, and lots of my other Jewish friends have similar stories about theirs. The interesting thing about kvetching is that you really only do it about the small stuff. When something really bad happens, even someone who is a constant practitioner of the art will become quiet and somber, and hopefully respond with poise and wisdom.

My mother's parents and my father's grandparents were big kvetchers. They all lived through terrible pogroms and other horrors when they were quite young, and for them kvetching was a way to deal with or not dwell on these past experiences.[1] They passed kvetching on to my parents, who had to deal with plenty of anti-Semitic challenges growing up in the 1940s and '50s in the United States. I also learned to kvetch, but honestly while I can't say I never experienced anti-Semitism, it wasn't anything like what my European-born ancestors had to deal with or even my American-born parents. Anti-Semitism just wasn't a constant, unrelenting day-to-day challenge in the life of most Jews growing up in the Boston suburbs during the 1960s and '70s. Yet I still kvetch like my forebears, and my wife will attest that it can be incessant and it's usually about nothing.

· · · · · · · · · · ·

Doesn't some version of the same thing happen to most of us? Don't we keep reacting to current situations based on previously experienced trauma, as if the same thing were still happening? Maybe we even pass it on to our kids or receive it from our parents. Maybe we are reacting sometimes to the painful experiences of our parents, instead of just seeing what is really happening now.

It's important, then, to know how to relax our subtle holding on to things—thoughts or hidden agendas or emotions. We don't need to worry about being perfect. We *can* have ideas, goals, and some sorts of emotional attachments and aversions, but we do *need* to be more relaxed about it. If we can relax clinging to our agendas and preferences, they won't be able to distract us. We will be able to be more fearless in chaos, and better able to be fully present. Then our efforts to help others and ourselves will be even more effective. We won't be waylaid by being too concerned about our hopes and worries. To relax the clinging, we use two exercises: Using Thoughts and Emotions as a Support, and Surfing the Wave of Impermanence. But before we go there, let's have a little story that will help introduce the point.

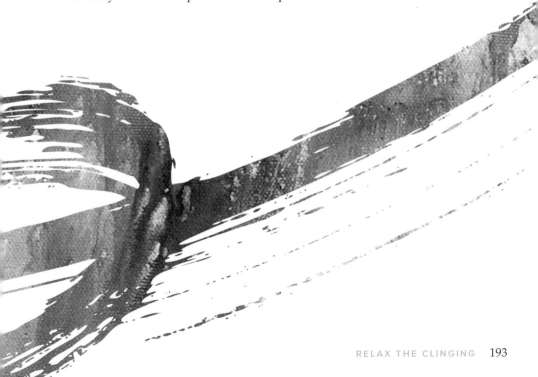

After my teacher told me to stop acting like a dog and to be more like a lion, I was a little bit embarrassed that my teacher thought I was like a dog. But as I looked at my own mind, I noticed more and more that I *was* acting like the dog. I chased every single thought, especially the angry ones!

So I went back to my teacher and asked him what to do. He said, "Instead of chasing the anger, grabbing it, and holding on, just be aware. Just be very gently aware of the anger instead of getting involved. Don't reject it, but don't dwell on it either. Just turn your attention to look gently at the thought. At that moment of turning inward to just observe, the thought will dissolve. At that moment, just exhale and rest. Then after a moment or two, it will come back. So just turn to observe it again. It will dissolve. Keep practicing like that and the power of the anger to ensnare you will be weakened. Then it will be

easier to forgive and, more importantly, forget. You won't be overpowered by the rawness of the emotion because you won't let it establish itself, you won't cling to it."

My teacher cautioned, "However, if anger arises, and you are aware of it, and it doesn't disappear, that means you are still subtly holding on to it."

I kept practicing, and gradually my anger became less and less powerful. I still would get annoyed, but I didn't feel like I had to punch someone or shout at them. I was a nineteen-year-old monk, and this practice saved me. Meditation made my mind much more flexible.

· · · · · · · · · · ·

Most people think thoughts and emotions are the enemy of present-moment awareness, and negative emotions in particular are the enemy of interconnectedness. But we can use thoughts and emotions, even the bad ones, to actually bring us into the present moment. We can overcome our negative emotions, not by rejecting them—trying to push them away—but by skillfully using them. Having thoughts is a natural consequence of having a mind. Since it isn't really possible to block thoughts, when we meditate we don't struggle against our thoughts by suppressing or blocking them. Instead we use an object to rest our attention on, neither pushing thoughts away nor engaging them further.

Rather than using an object such as the breath as a support for meditation, however, we can actually use the thoughts themselves. This is a more direct method for treating thoughts with equanimity. Using the previous methods, we may develop a subtle aversion to thoughts, since we kind of ignore them and stay focused on our object. We can develop the common misconception about meditation that *thoughts are bad*, which is absurd if you think about it.

In this method, we skillfully use thoughts themselves to bring us into the present moment. By learning to place our attention directly on a thought without holding on to it, we can use a thought as support for meditation rather than an opportunity for distraction. We just watch each thought as it rises and then falls away.

For example, when we go to the beach we notice everything going on there. Maybe a family is having a barbeque picnic or a group of teenagers is playing volleyball. Farther down the beach you might see a pair of lovers on a stroll. At that moment you don't feel like you need to get involved in any of the activity. You don't get up from your beach chair to cook burgers for the family having the picnic. Even if you like the game of volleyball, you don't just jump into the middle of the game and spike the ball to the opposite side of the net. And for sure, you don't knock one of the lovers over to steal a kiss from the good-looking one left standing, no matter how sexy that one looks in that bathing suit. You are aware of everything, yet you don't cling to any of it. You are not overly involved.

When we know how to look at a thought in meditation, without thinking further about the thought, our relationship to the thought changes dramatically. First of all, in the state of meditative awareness, thought loses its power to distract us, just as when we see a picnic at the beach we don't become involved in the picnic itself.

THE SPACE BETWEEN

There is also something else, though, that we gradually begin to notice when we practice in this way. Namely, when our meditation practice is a little bit stable and we turn our attention toward the thought, it immediately *dissolves*. A small space opens up between thoughts. In that natural space, we are still aware, still present and knowing, and we are not distracted.

At first, the space between thoughts disappears almost immediately because another thought arises to fill it. At that moment we can just turn our attention to that thought too and it disappears, just like the previous one. Gradually by practicing in this way, the length of time between thoughts slowly grows.

If we remain for a few moments in the natural space that sometimes appears between thoughts, in those moments we experience meditation *without an object*. In that space, we are aware, completely present, and not relying on placing our attention on an object. As we become more and more familiar with this state, the state itself becomes the support for the meditation. But in the beginning, we rest in the space between thoughts as long as it lasts—and for most of us this will be very short. But, when the next thought arises, we react with equanimity and just observe it.

A thought might bring us to non-distraction, but at the moment it dissolves, it is simply the non-distracted mind itself that is the support for meditation. Nothing else is needed. When we have confidence in the method, even challenging thoughts and emotions strengthen our dignity. They strengthen our ability to rest our attention on the present moment rather than succumbing to negative thoughts and emotions.

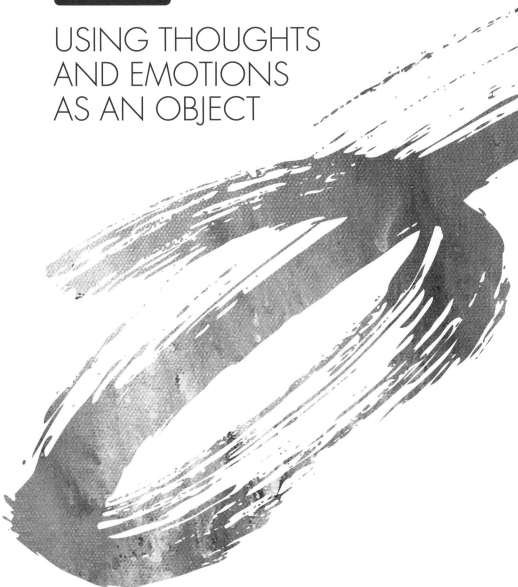

USING THOUGHTS AND EMOTIONS AS AN OBJECT

> If you have a hundred thoughts
> pass through your mind in the space
> of a minute, it means you have a
> hundred supports for meditation.
>
> —Gampopa

- Start by creating space.

- After a while, begin focusing on the breath.

- Notice what is happening in your mind; notice your thoughts.
  Don't think about your thoughts, just notice them.

- As a thought arises, just observe the thought. If you don't start thinking
  about it, the thought will dissolve. For a moment there will be natural
  space; just rest in it until the next thought arises.

- If you find you are thinking about thoughts, at that moment of recognition,
  turn your attention to the present moment.

- After a while, if you find you aren't able to watch a thought without getting
  involved in it, go back to focusing on the breath.

- End the session by considering your heartfelt aspiration for everyone to be
  happy, to have the causes of happiness, and to be free from suffering and
  its causes.

Continued overleaf

USING THOUGHTS AND EMOTIONS AS AN OBJECT

WATCHING THE RIVER

This practice is quite radical because, instead of regarding our thoughts as an obstacle to remaining in mindful awareness, we take the thoughts themselves as a support for resting in the present moment. However, in the beginning, thoughts and emotions may come so fast and furious that it seems like there's no space between them. That's because we have a subtle habit of clinging to each thought or emotion as it passes through our mind. In this case, practice "watching the river" by watching the flow of thoughts, rather than the thoughts themselves. When you look at a river, your eyes don't get distracted by each portion of water as it passes; it just flows by. The river is the flow. If there were no flow, we wouldn't call it a river.

In the same way, just rest your attention on the flow of the river of thoughts and emotions, instead of following each individual thought as it passes. That way you will gradually become accustomed to watching a thought rather than clinging to a thought, habitually thinking about the thought as it arises. By contrast, as we get used to watching the flow, the spaces between the thoughts will naturally reveal themselves.

So in this way, thoughts themselves become remedies for subtle involuntary thinking; they are an antidote to the unconscious habit of thinking about thoughts, which is just a kind of clinging.

- Don't cling to or try to follow each thought.

- Just observe.

- Whatever arises in the mind, just watch it come and go, lightly, and without grasping.

When you do this practice, you don't need to become like a cat waiting outside a hole for the mouse to show, ready to pounce. Don't wait, ready to pounce on the space between thoughts as soon as it arises. If you practice in that way, you'll succumb to thoughts such as "Oh, there is the space! I must rest in it," which means you are filling the space with another thought. The best is to rest in the space. Remain spaciously, whether there is any space between thoughts or not. Practice without any goal of finding a space. If a space comes, remain present in the moment. If a thought comes, remain present, observing it. Either way, *you are relaxing the clinging*.

You don't need to do this only during formal meditation sessions. You can do this practice almost anywhere, especially when you feel overwhelmed by too many thoughts. Just take a mini-break (page 94). It is good if you can first get the hang of it in formal meditation sessions, because then it will be easier to take advantage of a mini-break. But try taking a few moments during your day to look at a thought instead of clinging to it.

CHAPTER 12

By practicing Using Thoughts and Emotions as a Support, we get used to resting in the space between thoughts. In that naturally occurring space, there is no need for a meditation support (e.g., focusing on the breath), because we are fully present and aware. That space is usually quite short, but over time we become more and more stable in it.

There could still be a subtle problem, though: we may start thinking that thoughts are bad and we have to enter into a thought-free state to be really meditating, as we noted above. Or perhaps we feel we need a thought so we can look at it and then rest in its dissolution. Of course, when we think like this we are still under the influence of hoping for certain circumstances and fearing not getting them. Although by using thoughts and emotions as support we have begun to turn the mind toward the stone thrower, it is still a little indirect.

As we gain experience in meditation practice, we become more and more familiar with the awareness that notices whether we are distracted or not. We begin to see that we know we are distracted without having to have a thought such as, "Yikes! I am soooo distracted." The *knowing* quality of our mind does not depend on our thinking—we can be aware, know what is happening, without having to rely on thought. That moment of noticing that we are distracted is not based on *thinking* about whether we are distracted. That moment of knowing is a moment when we are free of distraction and fully present. In the beginning it may only last a few instants.

Like a lion not bothering to look at all the stones but rather turning to look in the direction of the stone thrower, instead of looking at the thoughts we can look at the maker of thoughts—awareness.

When you turn the mind to look at the knower of a thought, you are becoming like a lion looking at the stone thrower. At that instant of looking toward knowing, you can just:

let go and rest;

let go of being present;

let go of knowing.

At that moment of letting go, you are in mind's nature—awareness itself. The nature of mind—awareness—is always available whether there is a thought to be known or not.

What does it mean to let go? It means to just let the mind be, however it is. Don't concern yourself about whether or not you're noticing the knowing or if there is a natural space. However it is, just allow the mind to be that way. One way to think about letting go is to use the analogy of someone who comes home after a long hard day of work. After a long day at work, completely exhausted, they drop into their favorite chair and let everything go. So, just drop everything and rest like someone at the end of a long day of work. At that instant of letting go, you are aware, completely undistracted.

You need to have dignity to let go of clinging: the confidence that letting go is the way to practice, the confidence in knowing that what appears in the mind can be just like writing on water. When you write on water, it's there for an instant and then naturally disappears. When you cling to thoughts and emotions, it seems like there are all kinds of disturbances. But when you have dignity—the confidence to let go—there is no disturbance; thoughts and emotions naturally dissolve without any effort.

When anger arises, instead of chasing it, look at the knowing of the anger, let go, and rest. You can learn to practice that way in any situation, while completely engaged in life. Engaged, but not forgetting that it is just writing on water, remembering to look toward the knowing and letting go. You look at the anger and see the baseless aspect of the anger, then let go into the space of not finding any basis for the anger.

Anger is sometimes the thought "I am angry" and sometimes it is just an agitated, restless sensation in our body. Either way, we look toward the knowing of the thought or the knowing of the sensation, then let go. Our habit is to chase the anger, to get right into it, justifying the anger or rejecting the anger. So, we need to be aware of how it works, how the habit kicks into action.

When you are aware, you can catch the habit before it fully kicks in. Instead of habitually being like a dog chasing stones, you habitually become like a lion, using awareness as your object, rather than thoughts or emotions. When a thought or emotion comes, you naturally turn toward the knowing of it and let go.

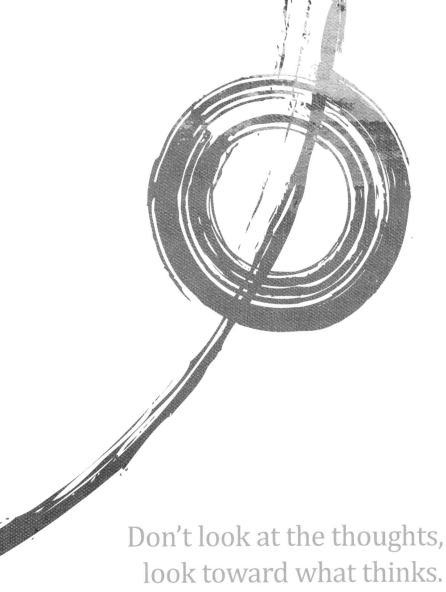

Don't look at the thoughts,
look toward what thinks.

—Tulku Urgyen Rinpoche

AWARENESS MEDITATION

This is meditation without the support of an object. We do not depend on any object to meditate, yet we are present and undistracted.

- Start by creating space.

- After a while, when you have settled into the practice, drop the method and allow yourself to be aware of whatever it is you are aware of. Maybe there is a loud racket outside the door, a fragrant aroma that entered the room, a tickle just under your shoulder blade, or even a rising thought.

- Now turn your attention inward, toward what is knowing the sound, smell, or sensation. At that moment, let go and rest within the natural space of awareness.

- Allow awareness to be aware of awareness.

- At that moment of turning toward knowing and then letting go, you are naturally present, not lost in thinking about thoughts. Awareness itself is free of focus, aware without being aware of something.

....

When you try to do this exercise, you may think, "I don't see awareness." But that instant of knowing you don't see *is* awareness. Otherwise, how could you know? It isn't that we are going to *see* some *thing* anyway. We just notice that we are aware. If we notice we aren't noticing that we are aware, at that instant of noticing, that *is* awareness. This practice is only difficult because we want to see something. But that subtle sense of noticing that you are aware is the very essence of radical happiness.

Awareness is always with us, from the moment we wake until we go to bed. Even in dreams we are aware. Awareness is with us in dullness—we are aware of our dullness. So when we practice like this we can be sleepy, looking toward what is aware of the sleepiness. We can also be agitated: we just turn our attention toward the knowing quality that experiences agitation. If there is no *thing* to be aware of, we turn toward the awareness that knows there is no object of awareness.

In this moment of awareness a thought might arise. As long as we respond with equanimity and gently turn toward awareness itself, the thought has no power to lure us away. This is true for sights, sounds, and smells too. Whatever arises in our mind, we don't struggle and try to push it away, nor do we begin to think about it. We just turn our attention toward what is aware.

ALTERNATING BETWEEN USING AN OBJECT AND RESTING IN AWARENESS

The moments of being able to rest undistracted without using an object can be quite short. If you didn't notice a natural space or a moment of pure awareness, don't lose heart. This happens gradually. Through regular and consistent practice, it gets easier and easier.

In the meantime, there is no need to struggle. It is usually helpful to alternate between meditating with an object and then dropping the method and resting your attention in awareness itself. Then, after a while, you return to using an object as support for your practice. You can keep alternating, a few minutes of using an object and then dropping the object and turning your attention toward awareness, then back to using an object and so forth.

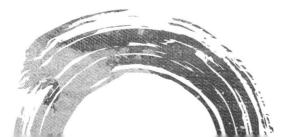

AWARE MINI-BREAK

You can learn to stop, drop, and be aware almost anytime, no matter what you are doing. When moving about, eating, talking to friends, or nearly any other activity, you simply take a mini-break, a moment where you:

- **Stop** following your thinking and notice what knows you are thinking,

- **Drop** clinging, let go, and rest in awareness.

- **Be aware**, by maintaining awareness of awareness.

It takes some time. You have to repeat this exercise again and again. But gradually, you will be able to integrate awareness into more and more of your life.

DIGNITY IN YOUR NATURE

As you do these practices, you will become more and more familiar with awareness—the nature of mind. This nature is not altered, improved, or stained by whatever appears to it. The capacity to know, even in dullness, is not made better or worse, by any thought, emotion, or sensation that is experienced. Clouds, rain, all manner of storms can appear in the sky, and yet the sky is never actually harmed or improved.

If you have a dirty washcloth, it may look like the dirt is part of the washcloth itself, and yet after the cloth is thoroughly cleaned, you can see that the cloth itself was never touched by the dirt. In the same way, as we become more familiar with our own natural awareness, we can see that although many negative, stormy thoughts and emotions might arise, the knowing quality of mind doesn't change.

This stainless quality of the aware aspect of mind is something you can gain confidence in. No matter what happens, there is a fundamental part of you that is never touched or harmed in anyway. By learning to focus your attention on noticing awareness, you can experience this stainless aspect of mind for yourself. Dignity in your nature is having confidence in the stainless quality, the method of noticing awareness, and the experience itself.

A DAILY PLAN FOR RADICAL HAPPINESS

If you have been working on the basic and interconnected happiness exercises, that's great. You will be able to draw on your experience for the radically happy daily plan. At the point when you begin to fully engage in a plan to be radically happy, you should be able to be consistent about practicing daily. This daily plan will need more of your time than the other two plans, since you are going to bring the practices of basic and interconnected happiness together. So it's best if you can spend about an hour a day on it.

······ RADICAL HAPPINESS ······

MORNING

Wake with awareness. As soon as you wake up, don't immediately jump out of bed. Instead, as the first moments of conscious awareness begin to take over from the world of dreams, notice how your mind is. Whatever thought, emotion, or sensation comes, as soon as you notice it, look toward the knowing quality

·

Morning meditation (20-45 minutes). Start by creating space (5 minutes). Practice Using Thoughts and Emotions as an Object or the Awareness Meditation (5 minutes), then practice Experiencing and Sharing Joy (5 minutes). Alternate between those two methods two or three times. End with two more minutes of Using Thoughts and Emotions or the Awareness Meditation.

AFTERNOON

Aware mini-breaks. Whenever you remember or you encounter your trigger, look toward the knower—or look toward the knowing quality of mind—and let go. After a few moments, make the aspiration for everyone to be happy (in three breaths).

Maintain your sense of awareness as you continue to do whatever it is you are doing. Don't forget to count your mini-breaks!

EVENING

Evening meditation. Start by creating space and then spend 10 or 15 minutes alternating between awareness and warmheartedness.

•

Review your day. Take an honest look at your actions: Were they in harmony with the interconnected nature of reality? Did you make decisions and act in a way that was more or less likely to have an authentic experience of yourself and the world? Is there something you can do to reduce the power of unhelpful habits? Is there a habitual response that keeps occurring, getting in the way? Can you begin to anticipate where it might arise? Imagine that tomorrow you catch yourself, and look toward awareness instead.

•

Reflect and celebrate. Reflect on how, despite a lifetime spent mostly chasing self-absorbed distraction, you spent time being aware. Celebrate the few moments you were aware, kind, patient, and generous or at least didn't succumb to habitual negative ways of reacting. Then visualize yourself doing it again tomorrow.

•

Sleep with warmheartedness. Get into bed with an attitude of gratitude that you made some worthy attempts to practice. As you begin to lie in bed, feel the present moment of awareness. Notice the sheets and blankets against your skin. Notice the knowing of the sensation and let go. Now just gently focus on your breath, mostly how it feels in your chest. Feel your heart. Imagine feeling a gentle warmth in your heart. Look at the knower of this and let go into gentle sleep.

AFTERWORD

Being radically happy is a lifelong, enthusiastic engagement with our mind, our heart, and our world. It isn't like a journey where we finally arrive at a nirvanic realm filled with light and laughter. In fact, by radically engaging our mind and heart in the present moment of warmhearted awareness, we will experience how we already have the ingredients for finding meaning and joy in our lives. Being radically happy is a process of uncovering what we already possess.

When you know this, any setback you encounter won't completely overwhelm you. When you hit obstacles you can still be content, because you know you are moving in the right direction. Being radically happy isn't a bunch of new rules to be rigidly adhered to. It isn't something to beat yourself up about. Of course, you will have bad days, when you see that you fell into old, unhelpful habits and negative emotions. But noticing that is in itself a reason to be joyful, and now you have a bunch of tools at your disposal that will enable you to gradually be free from the chains of ingrained habitual responses.

By practicing being radically happy, you'll develop a natural curiosity about how your mind works and where the habitual pitfalls lie. More and more you'll find the challenge of working with yourself in this way brings meaning and purpose into your life. So, regularly practice creating space and take stock. Ask yourself:

- Am I living in harmony with the interconnected nature of reality?

- Am I caring for myself and others?

- Are the decisions I am making, the actions I am taking, bringing me closer to authentic experience or not?

When we were finishing this book, Phakchok Rinpoche saw an unusual object sitting on the shelf in the apartment where we were guests. It was a snow globe, with the New York City skyline inside. He had never seen one before, so Erric picked it up and shook it, causing the snow inside to swirl. When he set it back down on the shelf, the snow settled and everything inside became clear again.

This is how our mind often is—a swirl of thoughts and emotions. But if we don't touch it, it will naturally settle and become clear.

The more we can live our lives according to radically happy principles, the more we will discover a natural lightness in our being. It is a gentle spark that infuses all our actions and makes us feel truly alive.

As this book comes to its finish, we'd like to leave you with a few simple aspirations.

May your mind become flexible, like flowing water.

May your actions be responsive to the needs of others,
like an experienced host helping guests.

May you maintain like space.
Space is immutable, it can't be harmed,
and within space things can appear.

May the light of happiness, this present moment of
warmhearted awareness, shine through.

ACKNOWLEDGMENTS

Many times a day I realize how much my own outer and
inner life is built upon the labors of my fellow men, both
living and dead, and how earnestly I must exert myself
in order to give in return as much as I have received.

—Albert Einstein

W e would like to express our profound gratitude for the kindness and patience of our teachers. They passed to us as much of the knowledge, love, and wisdom from the great meditators of the past as we were capable of receiving. Any insight that you gained while reading this book comes from them; the mistakes are surely ours.

In addition, there were many people who made essential contributions to this book.

Julian Pang, graphic artist extraordinaire, whose graphic realization of our words is an indispensable aspect of our work.

Norbu Gyari, who was indispensable in making sure that Phakchok Rinpoche's authentic voice was rendered properly in writing.

Eva Hopf, who in many ways was like another author, tirelessly working with us to develop the exercises and explanations throughout the book.

Barry Boyce of Victory Communication taught us a lot about the craft of writing a book. His work as our developmental editor graces every page.

Our agent, Stephanie Tade, was the first person who wasn't already our friend who really believed in this project. Her insights and encouragement were a constant source of inspiration.

The staff at Shambhala Publications helped us create the best book possible. We especially want to acknowledge our editor, Jennifer Urban-Brown, who spotted more than a few major problems, offered some important suggestions, and improved the book in countless ways.

There are many others whose kindness and insight helped make this book possible: Joshua Fouse, Jack De Tar, Michele Anthony, Matt Goult, Hilary Herdman, Oriane Lavole, Patrick Gaffney, Alfonso Schwartz, Mireia Petrus, Mathew Zalichin, Marcela Lopez, Maureen Cooper, John Makransky, Beatrice Zurlinden, Michael Friedman, Stephanie Wimmer, Jessica DuVal, Romy Pallas, Wouter Travecchio, and Pedro Beroy.

And naturally, there are other friends, too countless to mention, who have given us so much support over the years. You know who you are.

LIST OF EXERCISES

NOTES

CHAPTER 2
THE LOOKING-FOR-HAPPINESS CONUNDRUM

1 P. Brickman, D. Coates, R. Janoff-Bulman, "Lottery Winners and Accident Victims: Is Happiness Relative?" *Journal of Personality and Social Psychology* 36, no. 8 (August 1978): 917–27.

2 D. T. Gilbert, E. C. Pinel, T. D. Wilson, S. K. Blumberg, T. Wheately, "Immune Neglect: A Source of Durability Bias in Affective Forecasting," *Journal of Personality and Social Psychology* 75 (1998): 617–38, doi:10.1037/0022-3514.75.3.617. PMID 9781405.

3 Tom Meyvis, Rebecca Ratner, and Jonathan Levav, "Why Don't We Learn to Accurately Forecast Feelings? How Misremembering Our Predictions Blinds Us to Past Forecasting Errors,"*Journal of Experimental Psychology: General* 139 (November 2009): 579–89

4 Sonja Lyubomirsky, David Schkade, and Kennon M. Sheldon, "Pursuing Happiness: The Architecture of Sustainable Change," *Review of General Psychology* 9, no. 2 (2005): 111–31.

5 Matthew A. Killingsworth and Daniel T. Gilbert, "A Wandering Mind Is an Unhappy Mind," *Science* 330, no. 6006 (November 12, 2010): 932, doi: 10.1126/science.1192439.

6 There is a growing body of evidence that suggests mind-wandering is useful for certain kinds of creative problem-solving. For example, see B. Baird, J. Smallwood, M. D. Mrazek, J. W. Kam, M. S. Franklin, J. W. Schooler, "Inspired by Distraction: Mind-Wandering Facilitates Creative Incubation, *Psychological Science* 23 (2012): 1117–22. There are some suggestions that deliberative mind-wandering is more beneficial than the habitual mind-wandering: P. Seli, J. S. A. Carriere, D. Smilek, "Not All Mind-Wandering Is Created Equal: Dissociating Deliberate from Spontaneous Mind-Wandering. *Psychological Research* 79 (2015): 750–58, doi:10.1007/s00426-014-0617-x.

7 M. Csikszentmihályi, "The Flow Experience and Its Significance for Human Psychology," in idem, *Optimal Experience: Psychological Studies of Flow in Consciousness* (Cambridge: Cambridge University Press, 1988), 15–35.

CHAPTER 7
CONTEMPLATE THE INTERDEPENDENT NATURE OF REALITY

1   Dacher Keltner, Deborah H. Gruenfeld, and Cameron Anderson, "Power, Approach, and Inhibition," *Psychological Review* 110 (2003): 265–84.

2   George E. Vaillant, *Triumphs of Experience: The Men of the Harvard Grant Study* (Cambridge, MA: Belknap Press of Harvard University Press, 2012).

3   To heal childhood trauma, it can be a good idea to seek professional help, such as therapy. If this is the case, the exercises in this book will support the healing process. A good therapist is also a manifestation of kindness and care!

CHAPTER 8
RELAX THE JUDGING

1   J. Willis and A. Todorov, "First Impressions: Making Up Your Mind after a 100-ms Exposure to a Face," *Psychological Science* 17, no. 7 (July 2006): 592–98.

CHAPTER 11
RELAX THE CLINGING

1   A fun-to-read book on this topic is Michael Wex, *Born to Kvetch: Yiddish Language and Culture in All of Its Moods* (New York: St. Martin's Press, 2005); it's about how Yiddish is well suited to complaining, and complaining was a coping mechanism to deal with persecution.

ABOUT THE AUTHORS

PHAKCHOK RINPOCHE

Phakchok Rinpoche is a premier example of a new generation of Tibetan Buddhist masters. He combines the most profound aspects of traditional wisdom teachings with his pithy, humorous observations of their ongoing relevance to the incredibly fast pace of modern urban life.

Born in 1981 to a family recognized for their generations of spiritual accomplishment, Rinpoche was recognized as the seventh Phakchok Rinpoche and incarnation of a great teacher and meditation master. Receiving ordination from His Holiness the Dalai Lama, Rinpoche received a thorough education and training in Buddhist philosophy and meditation, studying with some of the most accomplished masters of modern times, his main teachers being his grandfather Kyabje Tulku Urgyen Rinpoche and Nyoshul Khen Rinpoche.

Rinpoche completed his education at the Dzongsar Institute of Advanced Buddhist Studies in Bir, India, where he received the Khenpo title. He is able to playfully combine the scholarly tradition of his studies with the experiential tradition of his main teachers in order to give his students the necessary tools to discover the wisdom and compassion that lie beneath our habitual ways of seeing ourselves and the world around us.

Now, Rinpoche travels the world, teaching in Buddhist centers, universities, and monasteries from Asia to the United States, from South America to Europe.

ERRIC SOLOMON

Throughout his career as a Silicon Valley technology entrepreneur, and now as an author and innovative meditation teacher, Erric has been interested in understanding the mind and how it functions, both as a user experience designer and as a mind hacker.

Erric's interest in human-computer interaction took shape when, as a teenager, he taught programming to children and school teachers. As a participant in the Logo Group at MIT's Artificial Intelligence Laboratory, he interacted with some of the world's deepest thinkers on how to make intelligent machines. This experience inspired a lifelong passion to understand the mind and how it functions, and it led Erric to the study of Buddhist theories of mind and the nature of consciousness.

He has been an invited speaker leading seminars and retreats in corporate settings—such as the World Bank and Silicon Valley tech firms—as well as in prisons, temples, and Buddhist centers across the United States and Europe.

ABOUT THE DESIGNER

JULIAN PANG

With the compositional brilliance of a true artist, Julian Pang has been bringing his clients' ideas to their ultimate graphical realization for the last fifteen years. An accomplished multimedia designer, Julian's out-of-the box approach has won him clients and acclaim far from his home base in Melbourne, Australia. Whether through illustration, calligraphy, graphical layout, or animation, Julian has the artistic eye, combined with a keen sensitivity for communicating with his target audience, to bring any design project from concept to reality.

Julian's images recall the old hand-drawn illustrations of the past yet utilize modern digital effects, resulting in illustrations that have the rawness and fluidity of natural media. This style is a perfect complement to the playful tension of the "Silicon Valley Technologist meets Old-School Tibetan Buddhist / Science meets Ancient Wisdom" perspectives that form the the basis of *Radically Happy*.